History of Fairfield County, South Carolina

By William Ederington

Windham Press is committed to bringing the lost cultural heritage of ages past into the 21st century through high-quality reproductions of original, classic printed works at affordable prices.

This book has been carefully crafted to utilize the original images of antique books rather than error-prone OCR text. This also preserves the work of the original typesetters of these classics, unknown craftsmen who laid out the text, often by hand, of each and every page you will read. Their subtle art involving judgment and interaction with the text is in many ways superior and more human than the mechanical methods utilized today, and gave each book a unique, hand-crafted feel in its text that connected the reader organically to the art of bindery and book-making.

We think these benefits are worth the occasional imperfection resulting from the age of these books at the time of scanning, and their vintage feel provides a connection to the past that goes beyond the mere words of the text.

As bibliophiles, we are always seeking perfection in our work, so please notify us of any errors in this book by emailing us at corrections@windhampress.com. Our team is motivated to correct errors quickly so future customers are better served. Our mission is to raise the bar of quality for reprinted works by a focus on detail and quality over mass production.

To peruse our catalog of carefully curated classic works, please visit our online store at www.windhampress.com.

C O N T E N T S

	PAGE
Introduction	1
Ordinaries and Probate Judges	9
Clerks of Court	8
Sherman's Army in the Rocky Mount Section	11
David R. Evans - Richard Winn	14
Revolutionary Soldiers - Lewis, Pickett, Gaither	16 - a
Sherman in Winnsboro	19
The Lyles Family	22
The Buchahans	28
Creighton Buchanan	33
W.W. Boyce	35
The Feasters & Colemans:	
Installment # 1	38
Installment # 2	45
Installment # 3	53
The Ederington Family	55
Various Fairfield Families	62
Some Prominent Fairfield Families	70
The Woodward Family	78
INDEX	82

****

From News & Herald, Winnsboro, S.C., Friday, May 3, 1901.

FAIRFIELD HISTORY

Representatives in Congress and in State Conventions -
County Officials -- Other Interesting items.

From EDRINGTON'S HISTORY

To the present and succeeding generations of Fairfield County I respectfully dedicate this little volume as a duty I owe to them in perpetuating the memories of a few of their ancestors, and as a token of my love to my native county.

The Author.

INTRODUCTION.

" Old people tell of what they have seen and done; children, of what they are doing; and fools, of what they intend to do."

As I am now perhaps the only one now alive. who knew some of the first settlers of Western Fairfield and a few of their immediate descendants, I may be pardoned for undertaking the ardous task of preserving for posterity the meagre knowledge I have retained of them from memory, besides what I can glean from "Mills Statistics of South Carolina," and "Woodward's Reminiscences." I am well aware of the fact that my homely phraseaology will not bear the inspection of the hypercritic, but as I write for the masses, I shall be well compensated if I can please them. The time has past to compile a complete historical biography pf Fairfield District, as important material has been lost by the death of the old settlers and no record kept of important facts. The reader will pardon the meagre account given of some men and families, as my knowledge of them being limited personally and historically. Where I have given full biographies, my correspondents furnished the material, or I knew them personally, or recieved my information from history. As I was born in the extreme Western portion of Fairfield and my correspondence limited in the middle and eastern portion of it, the reader will pardon the emission,

2.

in this work, of any mention being made of persons fully entitled to a record in history. The author will take pleasure in yet giving them a place in an appendix to the little work. But for urgent solicitations from friends I should not have undertaken this book at my advanced stage of life, and hope the readers of it will pardon any errors or omissions. The friends to the work have been very kind in furnishing material for it. I will here state that during my ilness I was greatly indebted to a young friend, a descendant of two prominent families spoken of in this work, for the interest manifested in copying my reminiscences, and letters from correspondents, relative to my book.

> "When I remember all
>   The friends, so linked together,
> I've seen around me fall
>   Like leaves in wintry weather;
> I feel like one
>   Who treads alone
> Some banquet hall deserted,
>   When lights are fled,
> Whose garlands dead,
>   And all but me departed! "

I shall begin by giving a few extracts from Simm's Geography of South Carolina.

"Fairfield was first settled by emigrants from Virginia and North Carolina. It derived its name most probably from the grateful appearance which it made in the eyes of wanderers, weary with long looking for a resting place. It is bounded on the north by Chester District, on the south by Richland, on the west and northwest by Broad River, which devides it from Union, Newberry and Lexington; aon on the northeast by the Wateree and Satawba Rivers, which sepatate it from a part of Lancaster and Kershaw. Fairfield is on an average 32 miles in length and 23 in width.

"The soil is very variuos, combining the best and the worse of the up-country. The lands on the water courses are rich and inexhaustible, cotton of the short staple variety, is much cultivated. The small grains grow well in Fairfield, wheat and oats in particular. The main rivers are the

Broad and the Wateree, both of them containing fertile islands, some of them in cultivation."

Fairfield has an inexhaustible supply of the finest granite for building; several quarries are now in successful operation. A branch railroad has been built from Rockton, a station three and one half miles below Winnsboro, on the C. C. & A. Railroad, running out about five miles in a westerly direction, to the quarried owned by Major T.W. Woodward, Co. James Rion , and Col. A.C. Haskell.

There is a remarkable rock not far from the railroad to Columbia, four miles below Winnsboro, called from its appearance, "Anvil Rock."

The population of Fairfield County in 1880 was 27, 765, the number of acres is 454,757.

Winnsboro is the seat of justice and the town of most importance in the county. It is a healthy and pleasant stop, thirty miles from Columbia. and one hundred and fifty miles from Charleston. It is on the dividing ridge between the Broad and the Wateree Rivers. The town stands on an elevation of more of five hundred feet above the ocean. The lands around are fertile , undulating and greatly improved.

By an act of the General Assembly, 8th of March, 1784, John Winn, Richard Winn, and John Vanderhorst were authorized to have it laid out as a town. It was incorporated December 20, 1832. Tarleton says that Lord Cornwallis, after learning of the defeat of Ferguson at Kings Mountain, selected Winnsboro as a place of envampment in October 1780. It presented good advantages for supplies from the surrounding country. He remained there until January 1781. His marquee was near the oak in front of Mt. Zion College. After inquiry , General Sherman in February 1865 placed his marquee on the same spot. During the Revolutionary War, a large military hospital was located on the premises now occupied by George H. McMaster and was used by both armies in turn. The British were buried in what is now the front yard, and the Americans in the rear. Mt. Zion College had its origin before the Revolutionary War. The Charter was granted on the 13th of February 1777, by the General Assembly then in session in Charleston, to John Wynn, Robert Ellison, William Strother, and others. The School was discontinued when Cornwallis occupied the town in 1780-81. In 1784, Rev. T.R. McCaule, of Salisbury, N.C. took charge of the school and a new charter was obtained in 1785. And then the foundation was laid for a large brick building, 44 x 54 feet, and two stories high, and cabins were built for the accommodation of boarders. "Afterward, during the administration of J.W. Hudson, under whom, from 1834 to 1838, the institution acquired a reputation so extensive within the limits of the Southern States, the building was greatly enlarged. First a three story brick building was added to the rear and then similar additions were made to the north and south side of the main building. This splendid structure was destroyed in May 1867 by an accidental fire, greatly to the grief of the community.

A one story brick building was soon after erected on the original foundation, at a cost of about 3,500 dollars. In 1878 a public graded school was established by the consent of the Mt. Zion Society, under the able management of R. Means Davis. This has been continued under his successors to the present time. In 1885, just one hundred years from the granting of the original charter, it was determined, if possible, to revive the collegiate feature of the institute and in connection with the graded school to furnish to the youth of our county the opportunity of obtaining a complete, practical education at home at a minimum cost. After various plans had been discussed and abandoned, a joint meeting of the Mt. Zion

Society and the citizens of the town was held, at which it was determined to issue bonds of the town to the amount of $75,000.00, for the purpose of erecting such additional buildings as were needed. Accordingly, on the 25th of May, 1886, ground was broken for the foundation of the large and well arranged brick building. This is just completed August, 1886, and contains eight large well lighted and well venilated school rooms, furnished throughout with improved seats, desks and all necessary apparatus. The Board of Trustees have recently elected Professor W.H. Witherow, of Chester, principal of the school. He was still principal in 1898.

As the Ordinance of Nullification, passed by a convention in Columbia, S.C., in November 1832, is a matter of history, I speak of it. It is said that there never was such an array of talent in our State before as was assembled in that body. Jas. Hamilton, Jr. was then governor of our State. Some of the members of the convention were Robert Y. Hayne, Chancellor Harper, Job Johnston, George McDuffie, Robert J. Turnbull, F.H. Wardlaw, Armistead Burt, Stephen D. Miller, John L. Wilson, Daniel E. Huger, John B. O'Neal, C.J. Colcock, John S. Richardson. R.W. Barnwell, R.B. Rhett, B.F. Perry, R.J. Manning and F.H. Elmore. The ordinance as to go into effect March 1, 1833.

There was widl excitement all over the State. The Buckhead troop of cavalry, of which I was a member, commanded by Capt. Thos. Lyles, who was afterwards promoted to the rank of Major, was ordered to be in readiness at a moments warning, to aid in carrying out the provisions of that ordinance. President Jackson issued what was called his "Bloody Proclamation" for the purpose of forcing our state to submission. Gov. Hayne issued one in ddfiance, declaring the State a sovereignty and calling on all good patriots to sustain him. It was fortunate for us that Henry Clay offered in Congress a compromise of the tariff act, which was accepted, reducing gradually for 10 years the duties on all imports to 20 per cent ad valorem. It was violated, and remained so ever since. The delegates to the Nullification Convention elected from Fairfield, S.C., November 1832, were William Harper, J.B. McCall, E.G. Palmer, D.H. Means, and William Smith.

The reader will naturally feel a deep interest in all that pertains to the late great Civil War. I will give a brief account of the Secession Convention and record the names of the members from Fairfield County who signed the ordinance. The Secession Convention met in Columbia early in December 1860, but smallpox appearing in that city, it adjourned to Charleston. The Convention passed the Ordinance of Secession December 20, 1860. The delegates to it from Fairfield were William S. Lyles, John Buchanan, David H. Means, and Henry C. Davis, men of firmness, sound sense and tried fidelity to the interests of their State. The first mentioned died April 1862, the second, the same year. Col. John H. Means was killed at the Second Battle of Manasses, and Colonel Henry C. Davis died of heart disease, Aug. 27, 1886, near Ridgeway.

There was a meeting in Columbia of the Secession Convention in September 1862, and in the election held to fill the vacances occasioned by the deaths of William S. Lyles and John Buchanan, William J. Alston and William R. Robertson were elected. The latter introduced in that body resolutions of regret, saying, "Since you all met together, Gen. John Buchanan, Maj. William S. Lyles, and Col. John H. Means have paid the last debt of nature and passed to the Great Beyond. The two former in beds of languishing, the last only a few days since on the plains of Manassas, on the field of battle, at the head of his command. All three of the deceased were natives of Fairfield District and gentlemen of marked character. Each of them filled posts of honor and distinction and had contributed to the social, moral, and political prestige of Fairfield." Col. Means had been killed so short a time before the meeting of the convention that there was no one sent to fill his place.

The reader will pardon me for saying I was a Nullifier and a Secessionist from Principle. I was a strict adherent of the doctrine set forth by Mr. Jefferson in his Kentucky resolutions, and an adherent of Madison's and John C. Calhoun's States-Rights Doctrines. We fought, but fought in vain, and though our banner may never again be unfurled,

> "He that complies against his will,
> Is of his own opinion still."

Fairfield is now entitled to three representatives in the Legislature and one Senator. This county has furnished the State with one governor, John Hugh Means.

The congressmen from this county have been Richard Winn, William Woodward, D.R. Evans, J.A. Woodward and W.W. Boyce. They served before the War. In 1884 Gen. John Bratton was elected to fill the unexpired term of John H. Evins, of Spartenburg, who died whilst a member from this congressional district.

MEMBERS OF THE STATE SENATE

S. Johnson, Samuel Alston, David R. Evans, A.F. Peay, J. Buchanan, N.A. Peay, E.G. Palmer, John Bratton, Henry A. Gaillard. and Thomas W. Woodward.

The Representatives in the Lower House of the Legislature before the War were: P.E. Pearson, James Barkley, William Bratton, John B. McCall, A.F. Peay, William Brown, J. Havis, Thomas Lyles, David Montgomery, I. Bonner, G.B. Hunter, T. Player, B.B. Cook, J. Buchanan,

J. D. Kirkland, J.A. Woodward, D. McDowell, D.H. Means, J.J. Myers, E.G. Palmer, J.D. Strother, W.J. Alston, O. Woodward, J.B. Means, J.R. Aiken, S.H. Owens, W.W. Boyce, J.T. Owens, W.R. Robertson, D. Crosby, H.H. Clarke, J.N. Shedd, R.B. Boyleston, W.M. Bratton, J.B. McCants, Henry C. Davis, and T.W. Woodward.

At the session of the Legislature in 1860 which called the Secession Convention, Edward G. Palmer was in the Senate and R.B. Boyleston, T.W. Woodward and James B. McCants in the House of Representatives. Of the Senators and Representatives who served before and during the Civil War, there are now but three alive: W.W. Boyce, now of Virginia; S.H. Owens, of Marion County, Florida, and T.W. Woodward, who is now Senator from Fairfield,

During and since the Civil War, Thomas McKinstry, Bayliss E. Elkin, W.J. Alston, J.R. Aiken, H.A. Gaillard, T.S. Brice, R.C. Clowney, A.S. Douglas, G.H. McMaster, John W. Lyles, C.E. Thomas, Charles A. Douglas, Hayne McMeekin and S.R. Rutland have served in the House of Representatives.

After the war, in 1886, Gen. John Bratton was elected to the Senate; in 1880, Mr. Henry A. Gaillard, and in 1884, Major T.W. Woodward.

These three have also been consecutively county chairman of the Democratic party since 1876; Major Woodward succeeding General Bratton in 1878. They have also been delegates to numerous State conventions. Major T.W. Woodward was for several years president of the State Agricultural and Mechanical Society; he was a delegate to the National Democratic Convention of 1872. Also, to the Taxpayers Convention, which made an ineffectual appeal to President Grant to relieve the State in her hour of dire distress.

CLERKS OF THE COURT AS GIVEN FROM THE RECORD

John Milling, from 1785 to 1793, 8 years
David Evans, from 1793 to 1797, 4 years

Samuel W. Yongue, from 1797 to 1828, 31 years
James M. Elliott, from 1828 to 1846, 18 years
A.W. Yongue, from 1846 to 1850, 4 years
O.R. Thompson, from 1850 to 1858, 8 years
G.W. Woodward, from 1858 to 1865, 7 years
S.B. Clowney, from 1865 to 1877, 12 years
W.H. Kerr, from 1877 to 1886 (present date)

ORDINARIES AND PROBATE JUDGES

D. Evans, from as far back as 1789, then John Buchanan from about 1800 to 1825; then J.R. Buchanan, James S. Stewart, G.W. Woodward and James Johnson. William Nelson was made Probate Judge in 1870, then J.J. Neil. O.R. Thompson was elected in 1876. J.R. Boyles was elected in 1878 and still holds the office.

John Milling is supposed to have preceeded James Muse as sheriff, then John Barkley, James Barkley, Hugh Barkly, Archibald Beaty from 1820 to 1824, William Moore to 1828, A.W. Yongue to 1834, Hugh Barkley (sic to 1838, D.G. Wylie to 1842, J. Cockrell to 1848, Richard Woodward to 1852, R.E. Ellison to 1856, Richard Woodward to 1860, E.F. Lyles to 1864, E.W. Olliver to 1868, L.W. Duval to 1875, Silas W. Ruff to 1879, J.B. Davis from August 1879 to December 1880, John D. McCarley from 1880, now in office.

It may not be amiss to here mention the hanging of Shadrach Jacobs. In the year 1809 or 1810, Ezekiel Wooley, a constable, had a state warrant to arrest Shadrach Jacobs, and while riding with Capt. Andrew Feaster towards and near Jacobs' residence, Capt. Feaster was killed by a rifle ball fired by Jacobs. The account given and proved in court in 1829 or 1830, twenty years afterwards, when Jacobs was tried and convicted of the murder, was that Jacobs had shot Feaster thinking he was Wooley. It seems that Wooley asked Feaster to change horses not long before the latter was shot, and it being near dusk in the evening, Jacobs could not discriminate between them, Feaster riding Wooley's horse. Jacobs absconded to the wilds of Georgia soon after the act was committed, and his whereabouts was discovered twenty years after and he was arrested and brought to Winnsboro, convicted of murder and hanged in 1829 by Sheriff Moore. In this instance was verified the truth of the lines translated from the German:

> "Though the mills of God grind slowly,
> Yet they grind exceedingly small;
> And patiently he stands waiting,
> Till with exactness grinds he all."

Although it was evident that Jacobs killed Capt. Feaster through mistake, yet his purpose was murder, and besides, his general character was that of a villian, and at the time of trial there was a requisition for his body from the Governor of Georgia.

****

From News & Herald, February 8, 1901

SHERMAN'S ARMY IN THE ROCKY MOUNT SECTION

The writer who tells of Sherman's march through South Carolina has a prolific as well as a sorrowful theme. Several days before the arrival of the army at Rocky Mount, February 22nd 1865, the southern heavens were covered with the smoke of burning buildings. Each day the smoke appeared nearer and nearer, and the hearts of the people beat faster. Next came a throng of fugitives, fleeing from their homes, endeavoring to save their stock and a few valuables. Then came straggling soldiers with many tales of woe and horror. Next was heard the skirmish near Gladdens, Then the smoke of the neighbors' buildings was seen in black columns ascending heavenward, then came the sound of the taps of the drums. The Yankee soldiers dashed up to the doors, gold and silver watches and silver plate were demanded, and whether given or not, the homes were throughly searched and everything they wanted stolen. Often when they did not wish the articles themselves, they took them and gave them to the negroes.

Yards were cleared of dogs. In one instance a soldier presented his gun to shoot a dog which had fled to its mistress' feet for protection. Had not an officer ordered him to desist, death might have been the result to the lady (Mrs. Robert Ford.) . Firearms were taken away and destroyed, a great many thrown into the Catawba River. The poultry was all taken. Bacon, flour, corn meal, corn and provisions of all kinds removed. Every locked door was forced open, gin houses and cotton burnt in every instance. This much was done by the first installment. Late in the evening they put pontoon bridges across the river and a part of the army went over in the afternoon of the 22nd. It rained and the water rose and broke the pontoons. By the morning of the 23rd the encampment reached from Caldwell's Cross Roads on both roads, to Rocky Mount Ferry. The six days and nights that the army spent there was a time of much sorrow and fear to the ladies and few old men who were at home.

Gen. Jeff C. Davis, of the U.S. Army, had his headquarters at the house of Robert Ford for twenty-four hours. He drove Mrs. Ford, her aged mother-in-law, and the children of the family from her room to an open portico to spend the night, an unpleasantly cold and wet one. He occupied her room, much to her discomfort. Gen. Davis travelled in a fine silver mounted carriage drawn by two fine white steeds, stolen on the march. His meals were served on silver waiters.

Gen. Sherman travelled through this vicinity on horse back, and save the wanton distruction of property, did nothing to render himself obnoxious. He had burnt ten buildings belonging to Mrs. Robert Ford, among them a large barn and stable. Several secret efforts were made to burn the dwelling house, but it was saved through the efforts of an Indiana private soldier, whose name I would be glad to mention if it were known. The family of Mrs Ford had a steadfast friend in the chief of artillery. He found some Masonic articles about the house and asked Mrs. Ford if her husband was a Mason. On being answered in the affirmative, he had the house and yard cleared of pillagers, gathered a few provisions and sent them in, and placed a guard over the premises. When he moved he left a paper which he hoped would be some protection, but here was but little left then to protect.

The Yankee soldiers shot down all kinds of stock, destroyed all farm implements and burnt the fencing. During the six days stay at Rocky Mount, they foraged the country for miles, going in squads of from four to ten, sometimes without arms. Gen. Sherman's headquarters were near the Barkley mansion. He treated the ladies in this section politely.

The neighborhood was so pillaged that the people for several days had to subsist on the gleanings from the camps. Mr. J.H. Stroud, of Chester County was very kind to the people in their dire distress. He sent an ox cart regularly with meal and flour. His name will ever be green in the memory of the unfortunate people of the Rocky Mount section. The good people of Bascomville, Chester County, and others also aided them. All aid received was from private persons. For two years the rations were mainly cowpeas boiled in water and a bit of cornbread. Without money, clothing or credit, there was real fear of starvation.

After the army passed, persons in the track of the march came and claimed all unknown stock and broken down and abandoned vehicles of all kinds. A few had some cattle left. They had to keep them under guard, or they would have been claimed and driven away.

Mr. Stephen Ferguson, of Chester County, an aged man, asked for a detatchment of Wheeler's cavalry, and came down and skirmished with the Yakkees in the yard of Mr. Robert Ford and Dr. Scott's, which greatly freightened the ladies. Ferguson rode boldly up to the window and told them to stand between the chimneys. He captured a few stragglers and left.

The army began to move actoss the river about ten in the night, seemingly in great excitement. Ferguson came with a large detatchment, but was too late. The army had crossed and the bridges raised.

****

From: NEWS & HERALD, WINNSBORO, S.C., February 19, 1901

DAVID R. EVANS ---- RICHARD WINN

(The following furnished by Col. Richard H. McMaster, 1661 Crescent Place, N.W., Washington, D.C., and is a re-write of Edrington's notes. The words underscored have been added by whoever edited the article, and may be of help to someone for further research.)

David R. Evans was the first lawyer in Winnsboro. He came to Winnsboro in 1784. He said that there were only three or four houses in the settlement; one, General Winn's, near where George McMaster's house now stands, the other a log college on Mount Zion Hill, Baker's Tavern, and perhaps one or two others. He was then fourteen years of age. His father came to this country from England, probably one or two years before they moved to this place. They lived in a house behind the one James R. Aiken recently lived in. He joined the Mount Zion Society and was secretary and treasurer for several years. His son, D.R. Evans, succeeded him in that office.

Mrs. Evans had her old English ideas as to manners, and was unpopular on that account. She was known to order a visitor to clean his shoes before entering her house. I know very little of the early life of D.R. Evans, Jr. He married first a daughter of General Winn. She died in 1806, and was buried behind the house in the garden. The tomb is still there, as well as the graves of two of Dr. Bratton's children, he having also married a daughter of General Winn.

D.R. Evan's second wife was a daughter of Parson S.W. Yongue. There were no children by either marriage. His second wife is buried at Jackson Creek. He died about 1845, and was buried behind the Aiken house, where his mother and father were buried. He had only one brother and one sister - Joseph, the father of a large family, of whom only Mrs. R.A. Herron survives, John Evans having recently died. Joseph's wife was a sister of

Colonel Jesse Davis.

An incident worth mentioning is as follows: About the latter part of the last century, a man named Baker had several wagons running, probably to Camden, which was then a considerable town. Baker got into a lawsuit and employed D.R. Evans. The other party employed a lawyer of Camden named Brown. Baker lost the case and was offended at something Brown said, and on his passing out of the Court House, cursed Brown for a "damned saddle-bag lawyer." Brown, being a samll man, could not fight Baker, but on going to his tavern he wrote Baker challange, which was referred to him by Evans for advice. Evans told him he would have to retreat or give Brown the satisfaction he demanded. Baker would have preferred a "fist fight", but finally accepted the challenge. The duel took place at Rock Creek Springs. Both were killed at the first fire. Baker was brought up and buried on his farm, two miles from Winnsboro. Brown was buried at Camden.

David R. Evans was a member of Congress in 1813-1814, Capt. Hugh Milling took charge of his affairs and physiced his negroes when sick. The old captain was severe on Generals Hampton and Wilkinson and others in regard to their conduct of the war with the British, saying that they could speculate in tobacco better than command armies. D.R. Evans was a venerable, gray haired man. I think he was about 75 years old, as I remember him, when he died. His only sister married Minor Winn, who was a son of Colonel John Winn. He was an unprincipled man, and Mr Evans induced his sister to separate from him. Mrs. Winn and her daughter taught school for some years on the General Winn lot, then owned by Mr. Evans. He at that time lived in his plantation where Mrs. Dr. Furham now lives.

Winnsboro was named for Colonel John and General Richard Winn. Col. John Winn was a high toned, honorable man. Col. John Winn owned most of the land around Winnsboro and lived at the south end of the town where Dr. Hanahan now lives.

General Richard Winn held the rank of colonel in the Revolution. He was a true patriot, and perhaps fought as many battles in the Revolutionary War and with as firm a heart as any man living or dead. He filled a seat in Congress of the United States for many years.

General Winn's family were not considered smart. Mrs. Winn's maiden name was Blocker, an Edgefield family. One of their daughters caused some merriment among her young lady acquaintances, who asked her where she got a fine shell comb she was wearing, by replying that "her father bought it in Congress".

Mills in his statistics of South Carolina, in writing of eminant men of Fairfield, says, "Gen. Richard Winn was also a native of Virginia." At the beginning of the Revolutionary struggle, he entered into the regular service of this state. Having acquited glory in the battle of Fort Moultrie, he was sent to the Georgia frontier, and commanded a company at Fort St. Illa. The service was a most perilous one and he was selected for it on account of his superior merit as an officer. Shortly after his arrival at the fort, he was attacked by a strong body of Indians and Tories. These he beat off for two succeeding days; on the third, he surrendered with honorable terms to Major General Prevost. at the head of a considerable regular force, suppered by his allies. (sic) General Winn returned to Fairfield after his defeat, if it can be properly called one, and to his command of a regiment of refugee militia. He was in several battles, and the success of the affairs of Hook's (Huck) defeat in York, and the Hanging Rock in Lancaster, greatly depended on his herpic exertions. At the latter place, said the great and good General Davis, who commanded a regiment of cavalry, when the firing became pretty warm, Winn turned and said, "Is not that glorious?"

16-a

He was wounded here and borne off the field about the time the enemy effected his retreat. On his recovery, General Winn continued to afford General Sumter his able support and ceased not to serve his country whilst a red-coat could be found in Carolina. He was a true patriot, and perhaps fought as many battles in the Revolutionary War, and with as firm a heart as any man living or dead.

General Winn moved to Ducktown, Tennessee in 1812, and died a short time after. And Colonel Winn and family, I think, moved to Georgia.

Winnsboro is remarkable for having been the headquarters of Lord Cornwallis in the Revolutionary War, after the defeat of Ferguson at Kings Mountain, where he retreated from Charleston. I was shown that part of the house in which Cornwallis was quartered, by Mr. John McMaster, who was then the owner of it. I was told by my friend, Dr. G.B. Pearson, many years since, that some of the most eminent men of South Carolina graduated at Mount Zion College.

****
REVOLUTIONARY SOLDIERS - LEWIS, PICKETT, GAITHER

William Lewis came from Virginia before the War of Independance, and settled in the vicinity of Rocky Mount, Fairfield County, where he continued to reside up to the time of his death, which occured at an advanced age, about fifty years of age. He was twice married and left a large family of children. For a number of years he was a member of the Methodist Episcopal Church. He and some of his neighbors, Picketts, Jacksons, and others, erected a rude log house to worship God "according to the dictates of their own consciences", after having been informed that if the Methodists continued to hold meetings at Shady Grove Meeting House, (not far from Flint Hill), they would be mobbed. A comfortable brick house of worship has taken the place of this rude hut, and Methodism still "lives, moves, and has its being" in this vicinity, and is the only church near Rocky Mount.

Mr. Lewis' record is good in the Revolutionary War. He was at Gates' defeat near Camden, was at Rocky Mount, Sumter's Suprise at Fishing Creek, Hanging Rock, and other places.

Some Tories had stolen a number of fine horses, and on a dark rainy night, encamped on the bank of Big Wateree Creek, on the plantation now known as LaGrange, and owned by Mr. John G. Mobley. William Lewis and a few others surprised them and captured the horses. The thieves had divested themselves of their clothing, save their shirts, and had them hanging around a fire, trying to dry them. They jumped into the creek, in this plight, and betook themselves to the woods.

On another occasion he chased a Tory and captured his horse and two sides of bacon which he had taken from a poor woman.

Reuben and John Pickett were Virginians, who settled on Wateree Creek. They aided William Lewis in some of the raids and skirmishes in which he engaged.

Richard Gaither came from Maryland, and settled in Chester County on Little Rocky Creek, but spent the greater portion of his life in Fairfield, where he owned a large estate of land and slaves. Much of the land still remains in the hands of his descendents. He died about sixty years ago (1826), at an advanced age, and his remains rest in the family burying grounds. We had no cemeteries in those days.

Mr. Gaither was also a Revolutionary soldier. He was confined at one time by the British in Camden, until he was nearly eaten up by vermin. His daughter, Rachael, obtained permission to take him some clothes. After accomplishing her mission, she and a neighboring lady who accompanied her, started on their homeward, a distance of forty miles through an unbroken forest. But the had not gone more than half the distance when a party of mounted Tories, who had no regard to passes , commanded the weary travelers to halt. As soon as Miss Rachel ascertained it was her horse they wanted , she bestrided the back of her fleet-footed animal , using her whip to good advantage, and after several miles of racing. she made good her escape . Her more timid friend gave up her horse and trudged her way homeward on foot.

On another occasion a squad of Tories came to her father's house and ordered a meal prepared for them. They were informed that nothing could be kept in the house for the British and Tories. Rachel's mother, after they had threatened her, told her daughter where she could find some coarse meal , and to prepare some bread and milk for them. When ready, she sat it before them , the milk in an old style pewter basin. After they had partaken of the bread and milk , Rachel told them that if the basin were melted and poured down their throats , it would be the desert of all others that she desired they should have. The lady has many descendants living in York County , - Bradshaws, and others.

SHERMAN IN WINNSBORO
March 8, 1901
News & Herald

On Monday, the day before Sherman was expected in Winnsboro, the citizens met and appointed a committee to meet the army beyond the limits of the town with a white flag in order to surrender the town. On this committee were Rev. Dr. Lord, Rev. J. Obear, James McCreight, and Dr. Horlbeck. The enemy came in early Tuesday morning, and Dr. Madden says he was near the town hall, and the Yankee soldiers seemed to rush in and suddenly fill the town. Their hands and faces in many cases smeared with sugar and syrup. One man stared in his face and said, "What do you think of our president now ?" On the farm of John McMaster, one mile below Winnsboro, the negroes were on the watch in the direction of Columbia for the Yankees, intending to hide out, but as they said, the whole face of the earth was suddenly filled as it were, by piss-ants as they said, so as to cut off any chance of escape. While standing near the town hall, Dr. Madden saw an officer mounted on a small gray stallion ride up and just then some soldiers brought up to him old Dr. Horlbeck, who explained that he had fought the soldiers and resisted an attempt to burn his house. The officer only said, "Speak quickly - talk fast," and rode off and replied to a question asked him, "Yes, I think all of the cotton will be burned, but it will be rolled out." Soon after that, fire was set to McCully's cotton warehouse, which swept Lauderdale's house and everything down to Levenstreet's brick building and crossed to the west side of the street and burnt from Odd (Old) Fellows Hall to the brick bank building. An officer said to Dr. M., "Why don't you assist in saving the movable property ?" He replied he thought the soldiers would not permit him to do so. All the houses in the tract of the flames were emptied of their contents which were moved to the lots in the rear. Three soldiers were standing near the court house yard talking. One said to Dr. M., "Do you know the lady who set fire to this town ?" Dr. M. replied that he did not know that a lady had done so. The soldier replied, "Yes, a lady did do so, and if we could get her, we would hang her to the highest limb of that tree." As two of the men walked off, the one remaining said, "You need not believe a word those men say. Nobody set fire to this town but our own soldiers. I'll tell you there are ten thousand men in this town who would take pleasure in burning every house in it." An officer on a large black horse rode up and said to Dr. M., " I am utterly opposed to this burning from beginning to end. It must stop." Saying, "I am General Williams." At that time fire was beginning to appear on the roof of the law offices in rear of court house. It was immediately extinguished . About noon on Wednesday, the 17th Corps under Jeff Davis entered town, and the Pennsylvanians lined the street of the northern end of the town. Some of them prized off the planks from the shutter of an outhouse next to Dr. Boyleston's residence, where a few bales of cotton were stored, and soon the flames burst forth and burned Dr. B's house, Miller's and John N. Cathcart's. An officer ordered soldiers to save the next house (Alex Chamber's house) and they ascended the roof and saved it, but the soldiers hurled imprecations upon them, crying out, " Remember Chambersburg ! " The cotton in rear of Charles Cathcart's house was next fired and by great exertions his house and that of Mrs. McMaster were saved. Dr. Madden says the soldiers expressed surprise at the great quanity of food supplies they found in Fairfield, saying it was the most bountiful county they had ever seen. They destroyed or carried off nearly everything. Many smokehouses

were some inches deep im molasses where they had destroyed the barrels and
other vessels that contained it.

****

THE LYLES FAMILY
March 15, 1901
News & Herald, Winnsboro, S.C.

I quote a paragraph from Mill's Statistics: " The first settlement of Fairfield District took place about the year 1745. Colonel John Lyles and his brother, Ephriam, were among the first settlers. They located at the mouth of Beaver Creek, on Broad River. Ephraim Lyles was killed by the Cherokee Indians in his own house; but by a wonderful interposition of Providance, the Indians went off and left Lyles' seven or eight children and his wife in it, after killing a negro on the outside. The Lyles were natives of Brunswick, Virginia, but removed to this county from Buis County, North Carolina."

By some it was believed that Ephraim Lyles was shot by Tories, not Indians.

Colonel Aromanus Lyles was the eldest son of Ephrain Lyles, and inherited all the land on which his father had located, by the law of primogeniture which was in force in South Carolina and other states until after the Revolution. He was a partisan officer during the war and fought in many of the battles. "Little Ephraim", as he was called by way of distinction, told me of his and his brothers being in the engagement at Fish Dam, where General Sumter commanded. and of other battles which I have forgotton, except that all of the Lyles, who were old enough, fought in the battle of Eutaw, which was one of the hardest contested conflicts of the Revolutionary War.

I think Col. Aromanus Lyles first married a Valentine, afterwards a Means, a sister of Colonel Thomas Means (she died childless); and last, a widow, Mrs. Kinnerly, in the year 1816. He died shortly after, in 1817. He had six sons and one daughter, viz: Ephraim, John, Valentine. James, Aromanus, Thomas, and Rebecca. Ephraim married a Miss Foot and removed to Chester District, on Broad River. He was captain of a militia or a rifle company before he left Fairfield. He was a fine looking gentlemen, even when he had ceased to be a young man. He had daughters, but no sons. The eldest daughter married a brother of Chancellor Harper (?) (papre torn and part missing here). After his death, she married Thomas Bookter, of the same county, by whom she had an only daughter, who died early in womanhood. Rebecca married Blanton Glenn. The youngest daughter married William Worthy, of Chester District, who soon after died, leaving one daughter, who married Capt. Thomas Bynum, who died in July 1884, at Glenn Springs. His widow and her mother are still living near Newberry Court House.

John Lyles married a daughter of Reuben Sims, near Mabinton, Newberry County. He had five sons and one daughter. The eldest, Benjamin, married Katie Rook; another son, Thomas Jefferson, first married a Miss Richarfs, of Union County, and had only one daughter. He afterwards married a Miss Harrington, of Newberry. His third and last wife was a Miss Earle, of Greenville. He died not long since, and was much loved and respected. His widow is still living, and married McGhee of Greenville. John, the youngest son, also died not many years ago. Eliza, the only daughter of John Lyles, amrried Golding Ederington in December, 1822. He died the following fall. and she married William Lyles, called "Carpenter Bill". He died not long after, leaving an only daughter. His widow lived until 1883. Valentine Lyles also married a daughter of Reiben Sims, and moved west. Capt. James Lyles married widow Goree. She was Drucilla Lyles before her marriage, a daughter of Little Ephraim. She had one daughter born to Goree, at the time of her second marriage, wh died in 1828. Capt. James Lyles was much respected by all who knew him he had three children, Ephraim, John and Drucilla; all are now deceased. He was a consistant, useful member of the Baptist Church for many years before his death. which took place in Mississippi, the state of his adoption. If not out of place, permit me to relate a story I have often heard years ago, to which Col. Aromanos Lyles was a party. It was that he was riding past a new ground. where an old Dutch woman named Margaret Godfrey was splitting rails. The Colonel, addressing her as Margaret,said: " Margaret, what in the devil are you doing ?" She replied, "I'se mauling". The Colonel responded, "Thunder couldn't split that log." She rejoined, "By G-d, I'se wus dan dunder." It was said to have been a gum log.

Thomas Lyles was the youngest son of Col. Aromanos Lyles (eldest son of the first settler of that name) and lived a short time after his marriage on Mill Creek, then moved to Wateree Creek, thence back to Broad River, where he was born, and settled on his father's plantation, where his father died in 1817. He next bought William Fant's place on the Columbia Road. and settled on it in January, 1821. He was a man of untiring energy and fixed purpose, of more than ordinary mental calibre. fond of mills and financial enterprises. With a large planting interest, he combined a mercantile enterprise and associated with himself John Smith, of Wateree. He commanded as Captain the Buckhead tropp of cavalry at the time our state passed the Ordinance of Nullification, and I was cornetist. We were all ready to march to Charleston to whip "Old Hickory", and would have done so, or tried, had it not been for the timely and fortunate modification by congress of the tariff act of 1832. I have often thought of the whipping we would have received had it not been for "Clay's Olive Branch", as it was so truly called. He was promoted to the office of major in 1832. Afterwards he was commissioned by Gov. R.Y. Hayne in 1832 as lieutenatn colonel of the 1st squadronn of cavalry organized within the 5th Brigade of South Carolina Militia. He was a true patriot. At the beginning of the late civil war, although he was seventy-five years old, he equipped a young soldier and sent him to fight in his place Major Thomas Lyles was a man of undaunted courage. At the time of Sherman's raid, he was confined to bed with a dislocated hip. One of the raiders, (perhaps thinking that he was feigning disablilty) approached with a lighted torch saying, "Unless you give me silver and gold, I'll nurn you alive." To this the old hero replied, "I have not many years to live any way, burn and be d---d." The Yankees, surprised at this characteristic speech, ordered a negro to remove the torch from under the bed, remarking, "You are the bravest man I have seen in South Carolina." Major Lyles represented Fairfield in the Legislature for eight years. He married Mary A.C. Woodward in December 1810. They had only two children, Thomas M. and William S. Lyles. His wife died in 1855. He lived at his home near Buckhead until his death, which took place on the 19th of January, 1874 at the advanced age of eithty-seven.

> "Life's labor done,
> Serenely to his rest he passed,
> While the soft memory of his virtues yet
> Lin er, like sunset huse, when that bright orb has set."

His older son, Thomas M., married Eliza R., the youngest daughter of Colonel Austin F. Peay. They were the parents of seven sons and six daughters; two of the daughters died in childhood. Mrs. Lyles died in 1897. William Boykin, the oldest son, was married to Sallie W. Strother soon after he returne from the University of Virginia. She lived but a short time. Two years later he married Georgianna C., daughter of J.M. Dantzler, of Orangeburg District. He was one of the first to respond to his country's call in the late civil war, and went from home as a first lieutenant of the Buckhead Guards to the attack on Fort Sumter in April, 1861. At the reorganization of the 6th Regiment, South Carolina Volunteers, in Virginia, he was made captain of the company and was killed at the battle of Seven Pines May 31, 1862, while gallantly leading his command to the charge, aged twenty-six years.

The enemy occupied the field next morning, and our men, sent under a flag of truce to recover our dead, were refused permission to enter the lines; hence he was buried on the field of battle.

> "But Freedom's young favorites sleep as sound,
> On foreign soil as native ground."

Captain Lyles possessed a warm and genial disposition, and was brave and generous to a fault.

> "When hearts whose truth was proven,
> Like his, are laid in earth,
> There should a wreath be woven
> To tell the world their worth."

He left a widow and one little daughter, Sue Boykin, who grew to lovely womanhood; married J. William McCants in 1882, and died six months after. They were not long severed, for he passed from earth November 1, 1885. Their mortal remains are interred in the cemetery of the M.E. Church in Winnsboro, there to lie till the resurrection morn.

Capt. Thomas M. Lyles had five other brave sons in the Confederate army, - Thomas, Nicholas, Austin, John and Belton. Austin was twice wounded, first at Dranesville, then at the Second Battle of Manassas, and was killed near Petersburg, Va. in June 1864, aged only twenty-one years. The four remaining brothers returned home unmaimed. Nicholas served through the whole war and was slightly wounded once or twice. Nicholas was sheriff of Marengo County, Alabama, ; died 1899. Thomas is living in Louisiana. Nicholas, who married Lou Poollnitz, of Alabama, moved to that state. John W., who married Sue C. Morris, is a practical farmer and was a member of the Legislature from this county one term. Belton married Rosalie McMeekin and James, the youngest son, married Cora Irby, who died. They all engaged in planting. Of Capt. Thomas Lyles' daughters, Sallie E. married Lieut. E.A. Poelinitz, of Alabama; Mattie P. married A.E. Davis, of Monticello; Rebecca V. became the second wife of Major T.W. Woodward, of Winnsboro; and Carrie E. married J. Feaster Lyles of Buckhead.

Old Major Thomas Lyles' second son, William, was a man of fine intellect, with a warm heart and generous to a fault; and like his father, represented Fairfield in the Legislature. He was an enthusiastic member of the Secession Convention. He died April, 1862, much lamented. He was twice married, forst to Sallie P. Woodward. They had several sons who died in childhood, and two daughters, Mary C., who married Colonel S.D. Goodlett, of Greenville, and died in January, 1877, leaving a son and daughter. Sallie P., the youngest child, married John C. Feaster, and resides at her grandfather's old homestead.

In May, 1846, Major William S. Lyles married Sallie A. Haynesworth, of Sumter Court House. There were five children by this marriage, Sue H., who married C.B. Pearson, and died in 1868; Fannie Hortensai, who died in childhood; Fannie Eliza, who died in her fourteenth year. William H., the only son, removed to Columbia, and married Miriam M. Sloan, of Anderson. He is engaged in the practice of law and has also been a member of the legislature from Richland County. The youngest child, Florence, married Mr. M.L. Kinard, a popular clothing merchant of Columbia, S.C.

****

THE BUCHANANS

March 22, 1901, News & Herald, Winnsboro, S.C.

Captain John Buchanan and his brother, Robert, came to this country from Ireland a few years before the Revolutionary war. Robert resided in Charleston and taught a classical school. He, with eleven others, secured the charter for Mt. Zion College in 1777. He was a lieutenant in the war and was captured at the fall of Charleston and died on a British ship.

Capt. John Buchanan raised a company in Fairfield, probably from the Scotch-Irish settlers; served in the battle of Cowpens and other battles of the Revolution. He was stationed at Georgetown, and at the landing of LaFayette, was the first American officer to welcome and entertain the gallant Frenchman who did so much to achieve the liberties of our country. He had the honor of presenting LaFayette with a fine horse. Capt. Buchanan had a body servant named Fortune. His name is attached to a spring in a fine grove near Winnsboro, where Fortune cultivated a rice patch. When LaFayette visited this country in 1825, Fortune went to Lancaster to see him. The sentinel at first refused to admit the old African, but he persisted, and was admitted by order of Gen. LaFayette, who recognized him and was rejoiced to see the servant of his old friend, Capt. Buchanan, though near fifty years had elapsed since Fortune had blacked his boots. This is not the only time Fortune appeared in public. It is said that during the French Revolution, the Captain inspired by gratitude towards France, and dislike for England, sometimes on public occasions, when full of military enthusiasm and good brandy, would don his continental uniform, mount his war steed, and followed by Fortune, his body guard, would ride up and down the main street of Winnsboro, to the admiration of old Whigs and the patriotic youth of the town.

Some years afterwards, the Captain converted to Methodism by "Thundering" Jenkins, a stalwart preacher of the day, abandoned the unholy ways of his youth, and with William Lewis and Major Henry Moore, built the old square brick Methodist church in Winnsboro. In passing, the writer will state that in a copy of Ramsey's History of South Carolina, which was in the town library about 1848, he read in penciled notes, on the battle of Stono, made by Major Moore, that he himself manned one of the cannon at that battle at which time he was ensign. The old Major lived near Winnsboro, and died in 1840.

Captain John Buchanan possessed high ability and character conjoined with much personal dignity. He was precise in his manners, and careful in his apparel. His portrait which hangs in G.H. McMaster's parlor is said to be a fine likeness of him and has the appearance of an old style first class Methodist bishop. He, to the close of his life, wore knee breeches, stockings, and silver buckles on his shoes. He held several important Federal offices, and was judge of ordinary during his life. John R. Buchanan, his nephew, a gentleman of great worth and piety, succeeded him as ordinary, and held it during his life. Capt. John Buchanan kept a house of entertainment for some years and in 1805 he turned it over to his brother, Creighton Buchanan, and returned to a brick house which he built on the hill. Early in the century he induced his brother William's family to emigrate to Winnsboro, consisting of the widow, her son, John R., one daughter who married James McCreight, one (sic), the Rev. Wm. Carlisle, whose sons, Prof. James H. Carlisle and Capt. John Carlisle, now reside in Spartanburg; and a *Rev.*

who married John Lewis.

He had no children. He married Sallie Burney Milling, the widow of David Milling, whose two daughters, Sarah and Mary, married Thomas and John Means, two young men from Massachusetts, but of Irish parents, whose descendants in Fairfield have been honored for their ability, courage, kindness of heart and hospitality. Capt. Hugh Milling, brother of David Milling, was another noble soldier of the Revolution.

Capt. B. died in 1824, aged 74. His remains rest near the church of which he was the chief founder.

GEN. JOHN BUCHANAN,

the eldest son of Creighton Buchanan, was born on Little River, near Buchanan's Ford, in 1790. He received his academic education at Mt. Zion College, and graduated at the South Carolina College in 1811. During the War of 1812 he was adjutant of a regiment in and around Charleston. His first uniform was spun, woven and made by his sister, Rachel. The wool sheared, was then woven and the suit made in one week. This time, except in rare instances, all articles of clothing were the product of home industry among the people of Fairfield. After the declaration of peace, Gen. Buchanan taught school at Sillisonville, then returned to Winnsboro, studied law with Capt. Clark, and was his partner for some years.

He afterwards held the office of commissioner in equity. He inherited considerable property from his uncle, Capt. John Buchanan, and combined planting with the practice of law. As a lawyer he stood for years at the head of the bar. He was a good student and had one of the best libraries - legal and miscellaneous - in the up-country. His style of speaking was entirely argumentative. He had no rhetorical flourishes or graces of oratory, but such was the confidences in his spotless integrity that he was generally successful in his cases.

The War of 1812 renewed the military spirit which had begun to wane after the Revulotion, and there was great ambition among young men to attain military honors. The young captain was full of the military enthusiasm of the day and was soon promoted to the highest military position of Major General, which he held to the end of his life. His competitor was General Blair, of Camden, the Congressman who subsequently committed suicide while attending a session of Congress.

When General Buchanan first went to the bar at Winnsborough (as it was then spelled), there were very few men in the district who had the advantage of a college education. The only graduates of colleges at that time in the district were Samuel C. Berkley, David, Robert and Thomas Means, John B. McCall and E.G. Palmer, Wm. Woodward, Robert Barkley and N.P. Cook, who left college before graduation. General Buchanan came into public life a few years after the great senatorial contest between Samuel Johnson, whose supporters were Scotch-Irish, and James Alston, the father of Wm. J. Alston, whose followers were the Virginians and the country born.

Party spirit ran high, but the Scotch-Irish and their descendants sent Samuel Johnson to the Senate.

The War of 1812 fused all the discordant elements, and General Buchanan, a young soldier and a graduate of the State College, and liked by his numerous kinsfolk and connections, most of whom were well-to-do farmers and substantial Presbyterians, soon came to the front, and in 1832 we find him a leader in the cause of nullification. He maintained his great popularity for a longer period than any other man has ever done in Fairfield District. For more than a quarter of a century he represented his people in the State Legislature. He was a splendid electioneerer. He would ride in his sulky from house to house, stop with his friends, and discourse on subjects that were generally instructive. His talks were frequently illustrated by references to books of learning. His historical al-- and apparent knowledge in its departments , combined with a dignity which never forsook him, gave him a reputation of being wise and profound. Indeed, when his habit of drinking seemed to threaten his usefulness, it was frequently remarked by his friends that they would rather have the old General in spite of his failing, than any other man in the district.

His conduct in every other respect was exalted . No one ever heard a profane word from his lips , and he had the greatest contempt for any one who related a vulgar ancedote. His standard of duty was elevated, refined and without reproach. He had a supreme disdain for the arts which is the chief stock in trade of most politicians of the present day.

General Buchanan married Harriet Yongue, a daughter of old Parson Yongue, who came to Winnsboro from North Carolina in the last century; taught at Mt. Zion, and preached at Jackson Creek and Wateree churches. His eldest son, John M., lives in Texas; Samuel, his second son, died at 25 years of age. He was an excellent gentleman and a superb orator. When Hon. W.C. Preston heard of his death , he exclaimed, " The Commonwealth has sustained a great loss."

General Buchanan's third child was Ann, who married Rev. Edward Palmer, who is now a Presbyterian preacher in Louisiana. His youngest son. William Creighton, graduated at the South Carolina College in 1852. He was brave, kind hearted and true. He studied law, went to Kansas to engage in the prospective fights with the Free Soilers and spent two years there. When the Confederate War broke out he was made adjutant of the 12th South Carolina Volunteers and fell , mortally wounded in the battle of Chantilly in 1862. General John Buchanan was a great advocate of learning, a strong supporter of Mt. Zion, and lavished money in bestowing upon his children the advantages of a high education. He died in 1862.

CREIGHTON BUCHANAN

was too young to accompany his brothers, John and Robert, to America before the Revolution.

He with his wife Mary Millikem, settled in 1789, on land belonging to his brother John, now owned by Ed. Robinson, near Little River. In 1795 he moved with his wife and children, John, Rachel and Martha, to a place near Jackson Creek church; the church at that time was being built of rough unhewn stones. His mother, who lived with him, died and was buried on the west side of Jackson Creek below the Milling burial ground. He afterwards bought the farm on Little River, now owned by T. Herden. In 1805 he removed to Winnsboro and bought his brother John's tavern. Capt. Hugh Milling and Capt. James Phillips, uncle of Creighton Buchanan, lived near by on the east side of the road, leading from Belle's bridge to Columbia. General R. Winn lived on the place now occupied by W. Turner.

Jas. Phillips was a loyalist, though a Scotch-Irishman, who almost universally were rebels. A large proportion of Marion's men were Scotch-Irish, and the history of the county is illustrated by their deeds. The captain had the good fortune never to meet any of his kindred in battle, who were all rebels, being assigned to command at St. Augustine, where he remained during the whole war. He lived in Charleston, but after 1776 his wife with her sons, Smith, Robert, and James, moved to Jackson Creek among her kin. James lived to a good old age, and was a school-master and county surveyor.

When Capt. Phillips returned home after seven years absence, his wife, for a time, refused to be reconciled to him. The Captain being a gentleman of culture and of high moral character, soon mitigated the hospitality of his neighbors and lived for many years highly respected. He, Gen. Winn and Capt. Hugh Milling were boon companions and met almost daily at each others houses to read the newspapers and discuss literary and political matters. His elder brother, Colonel John Phillips, also being a Tory, was put in command at Winnsboro when Cornwallis left. He was a just and humane man. At different times he saved the lives of Whigs who were about to be executed by the order of Cornwallis, among them being Colonel John and Minor Winn, and he always endeavored to check the rapine and cruelty of his followers.

At the close of the war, he learned that one of his daughters was about to marry a Mr. McMullin at a church in Charleston where he lived. He rushed to the church, forcibly took his daughter, and with his family went back to Ireland. Colonel Phillips was a man of wealth and education, and on his return to Ireland, he was appointed a pension officer and held it for life.

Creighton Buchanan spent his last days on his farm, now owned by McCants, near Winnsboro. He was a quiet, intelligent and devout man, and was much respected by his neighbors. He left surviving him by his **first** marriage, Gen. John Buchanan, Mrs. Rachel McMaster; Martha, a **brilliant** young lady, had died at 18 years of age. The children of his second wife were Eliza, who married J. McKinney Elliott; Robert, who is now a retired physician residing in Winnsboro, and Calvin, who removed to Texas in 1844. Creighton Buchanan died in 1823, aged 63.

****

W.W. BOYCE

From Edrington's History of Fairfield.

News & Herald, Friday, May 10, 1901

- - - - - - - - - - - - -

John Boyce, grandfather of W.W. Boyce, came from Ireland. In 1765 he settled in Newberry County, South Carolina. He had one brother, Alexander Boyce, who commanded a company of artillery in the Revolutionary War, dying gallantly in the service of his country during the siege of Savannah. He was a merchant of Charleston. The Boyces went to England at the time of the conquest; they afterward settled in the north of Ireland and were staunch Presbyterians.

William Waters Boyce was born in Charleston, South Carolina, October 24, 1818; his parents were Robert Boyce and Lydia Waters, both natives of Newberry. The Boyces are of Norman descent and came to America from Ireland. The first Waters who came over, came in the "Mayflower." Both Boyces and Waters fought bravely in the Revolutionary War. The mother of Mrs. Lydia Waters Boyce was Ruth Llewellyn, who claimed descent from Griffith of Llewellyn, the last of the Welsh kings.

William W. Boyce studied both at the South Carolina College and Virginia University, at both of which he ranked with the talented young men. In October 1838, he married Mary E. Pearson, daughter of Dr. George B. and Mrs. Elizabeth Pearson. He began the practice of law in Winnsboro, South Carolina in 1841. He served in the South Carolina Legislature on term, 1846 and 1847. In 1850 he was prominent as a co-Operationist in the famous secession contest of that year. He was elected to the United States House of Representatives in 1853. .. December 1860 (part of paper missing) -- always listened to with marked attention by both sides. He was the most conservative Southern man in Congress. His report on Free Trade, he being chairman of the special committee to which it was referred, created a worldwide sensation.

Richard Cobden, the great English Free Trader, thus wrote of it: "I can conscientiously say that I have never before enjoyed the pleasure of reading so condensed and yet so complete an argument in favor of Free trade and Direct taxation."

Mr. Boyce always regretted secession, but went heartily with his State. He was never sanguine of the success of the Southern cause, though as a member of the Confederate Congress he always urged active measures. He grieved over the sad spectacle of his sorrowing country, the precious lives lost and general financial ruin. In the autumn of 1864, he wrote and published his letter to President Davis on the subject of peace. A storm followed, but he was sustained by an inner consciousness of duty performed and the sympathy of men from all sections of the Southland. Within the past year a very decided letter from General Lee on the same subject was made public for the first time. This letter was written in June, and that of Mr. Boyce in September, 1864. Mr. Boyce possessed more moral courage than any public man in the South during that troublous time. He had convictions, and courage enough to express and maintain them. Had he lived in a wiser age, he would have been more appreciated.

The ending of the war left Mr. Boyce impoverished, most of his best years were devoted to the public, and his own affairs neglected, consequently, he was forced to begin life anew.

In December, 1866, he left South Carolina, accompanied by Mrs. Boyce, and settled in Washington, D.C., for the purpose of practicing law, but owing to the "test oath", it was several years before he was allowed to appear in the courts, during which time he assisting in editing the National Intelligence, corresponded with several other papers and assisted General Caleb Cushing in his practice.

There was something quite pathetic in his struggles at this time, but throughout he was cheerful and industrious. At last a brighter day dawned, and restrictions were removed, and Mr. Boyce began his practice befroe the commissions and United States Courts, and although he has not amassed wealth, he has a competence and is forced to work no longer. He lends leads a quiet, uneventful life at his country home in Fairfax County, Virginia. His household consists of Mrs. Boyce, her sister, Mrs. Herbert, his son-in-law, Richard W. Gaillard, and only daughter, Frances B. Gaillard.

**** **********

THE FEASTERS AND COLEMANS.

(From Edrington's History)

News and Herald, Winnsboro, S.C., May 17, 1901.

Andrew Feaster (the name was then spelt Pfister, 1740) emigrated to this State from Bucks County, Pennsylvania. His father, Peter Feaster, died on the road and was buried somewhere in Virginia. From his was descended the present family of Feasters on the Beaver Creek section of the county, better known as the Feasterville township. He had a cousin, John Feaster, who came at the same time and settled in Edgefield County. He was the great-grandfather of Laurens Feaster of the "Dark Corner" section.

Andrew Feaster was twice married; by the first wife only one daughter, who married William Colvin, of the Sandy River section of Chester County, now known as the Halsellville township, near where John Simpson now lives. She moved with some of the children to Greene County, Alabama, and lived to be quite an hundred years of age. His second wife was Margaret Fry Cooper, who had by a former marriage, two children, Adam and Eve Cooper, both of whom lived to be quite old. Eve married Jacob Stone, whose mother was Ruth Lyles, a member of the Chester branch of that family. Jacob Stone was a soldier in the Revolution and drew a pension as long as he lived. Andrew Feaster's children by the second marriage were: John, who married Drucilla Mobley, daughter of Samuel Mobley. She died 1806 (actually Drucilla died April 15, 1807). John's children were: Jacob, better known as "Squire Jake", Andrew, Savilla, Susan, Mary, Cheney, and John M. Savilla married Robert Gregg Cameron, and now lives near White Oak. John M. married Keziah Pickett. He now(1886) is living in Florida, on Indian River. Jacob, son of John, married Isabelle Coleman, daughter of David R. Coleman, than whom a better man never lived. Jacob Feaster lived and died near Buckhead. His children were: Jacob F., who married Elizabeth Stone. Moses C. Feaster is the only living child of that marriage.

Edith D. married Henry J. Lyles. They had four children, three of whom are now living. John C. married Miss Sallie Lyles, youngest daughter of the late Col. William S. Lyles, by his first marriage to Miss Woodward. Susan E. married S.M. Simons, of Lexington County, South Carolina. David R. married Miss Victoria E. Rawls of Columbia, S.C., by whom he had several children. His first wife died in January, 1877, and in December, 1878, married Mrs. Hattie E. Coleman, nee Porter, a daughter of Rev. C.M. Porter, of Ridgeway, South Carolina. By her former marriage she had five children. By her marriage to D.R. Feaster, she had four. They have one of the largest families in the county. Sixteen children and six grandchildren. There were two girls younger than D.R., Isabelle and Mary N., both of whom died quite young.

Andrew Feaster, John Feaster's second son, married Mary Norris of Edgefield County, by whom he had eleven children, 5 sons and 6 daughters. The youngest son, T.D. Feaster, is now living near the old homestead. He is the only one of this family now living in this county. The eldest son and daughter are living near Columbia. The fourth son, Elbert H., was blind from infancy, and was educated at Boston, Mass. He was a remarkable man. He knew every one by their voice. Once having been introduced and conversing with the verist stranger, he would ever after know him by his voice, no matter where he met him.

Nathan A. Feaster, second son of Andrew, was thrice married; first to Maria Louisa Rawls, of Columbia, by whom he had one daughter, who married John G. Wolling, of Feasterville. His second wife was a Miss Brown, of Anderson County, a sister of Col. Newton Brown, by whom he had one daughter, who is now the wife of a Mr. Tribble, of the town of Anderson. His third wife was a Miss McClanahan, of Greenville County. There are two children by this marriage now living in Greenville, a son and daughter. Jacob N., Andrew's third son, was twice married, and is now living in Florida. The eldest daughter married Dr. T.J. Rawls, of Columbia. The doctor is dead, and Mrs. Rawls and her only child, B.A. Rawls, are now living in Columbia.

The second daughter married William Williams, of Anderson County, and moved to Texas, since the war, and there died. Belle, the third daughter, married William Lonergan, of Charlotte, North Carolina, by whom she had several children, only one now living, the wife of G.W. Coleman. Julia, the fourth daughter, married Robert H. Coleman, who died at Augusta, Georgia, during the late war. Mrs. Coleman now lives in Florida. Sallie, the prettiest of all the girls, married George Butler, and died without issue. Narcissa M. Feaster died a few years since, unmarried. Susan, John Feaster's oldest daughter married Robert F. Coleman, a son of the Patriach, D.R. Coleman. Mrs. Wesley Mayfield is the only one living of that family. The second daughter, Mary, married H. Jonathan Coleman, by whom she had sixteen children, eleven of whom lived to be grown, 9 sons and 2 daughters. Truly may it be said that Feasterville township was benefited by the issue of this marriage. It gave to the township three of the very best physicians, two of whom, Drs. Preston and Franklin Coleman, gave up their lives in Virginia for the "Lost Cause." Only two of the boys are now living, D.R. Coleman, of Feasterville, and G.W. Coleman, of Cash's Depot, South Carolina. Allen lost his life at Petersburg; Jacob died at Wilmington, N.C., in 1864; Dr. R.W. Coleman, better known as "Dr. Bob", was one of the best nurses that ever lived. He married Nancy McConnell, by whom he had several children. He was as game as a Ku Klux to the day of his death, which occurred in May, 1873. John Feaster, the eldest, married a Miss Gladden and died in February, 1856. His wife died April following, leaving six small children to the cold charities of the world. But the noble old Roman, H. Jonathan Coleman, was equal to the occasion. He and his married children took these orphans and raised them in their families as one of their own children. H.J. Coleman, Jr., died in May, 1874, leaving a wife and five children. His widow is now the wife of D.R. Feaster. Dr. Preston Coleman married a Miss Secrest of Lancaster. He was captian of Company C, 17th South Carolina Regiment and had his leg shot off at the knee at the second Battle of Manassas. He and Dr. B.F. Coleman were educated at The Citadel Academy. Dr. B.F. was Lieutenant of his brother's company. He was wounded and died a few months after at Winchester, Va., where his body now lies. D.R. Coleman had his eyesight impaired by a blast during the construction of the S. & U. Railroad. G.W., the youngest son, went to the front at the age of 17. Elizabeth married Beverly C. Mitchell; both living in Americua, Ga. Johnn Feaster daughter, Chaney, married H.A. Coleman. There were eight children by this marriag only three now living: J.A.F. Coleman is now living at the old homestead, a man of high social qualities and industrious habits. He is better known by the sobriquet of "Beeswax"; David A. Coleman married Sarah A. Yongue, who survives him, he havin died during the war. She has reared as noble a family of boys as there is in Feasterville Township. J.A.F. Coleman married a daughter of Samuel H. Stevenson, who lives in the hearts of his neighbors and friends, and everybody knows "Uncle Sam", and it will not be left to the futures generations to do so, but the present one calls him blessed. Henry A. Coleman married Rebecca Younge. He was wounded three times at the Second Battle of Manasses, and did not live long after, leaving an only daughter, now living with her mother in Winnsboro, S. C.; Robert C. Colema the youngest son of "Uncle Henry's" was drowned while bathing at Church Flats in 1

The eldest daughter married William Younge, son of Robert Younge. The second daughter married James Levy Hunter, of Chester County, but now of Powder Springs, Cobb County, Georgia. Isabelle, the third daughter, married Thomas L. Manning of Marietta, Georgia. The fourth daughter married A. J. McConnell, better known as "Dick." She died a short while after her marriage. He was first lieutenant of Bailey's Company, 17th Regiment, and was killed the day of the "blow up" at Petersburg. John Feaster's youngest daughter, as has been mentioned before, married R. Gregg Cameron. She raised seven sons and four daughters; James, the eldest, emigrated to Florida to look after the interests of John M. Feaster, whose daughter he afterwards married. He died not long after, leaving a widow with one child. John married Mrs. Hoffman, nee Robinson. She did not live long, and John died in Columbia, 8 or 10 years ago.

J. Feaster Cameron was a man of education and refinement, a nobleman of the day. He was colonel of an Arkansas regiment, was twice shot and left for dead, but he was spared to be a living witness to the destroying power of ardent spirits. He was one of the best of lawyers, a hero of many battles, that fell a victim to our nation's curse, strong drink. The second son, Dr. Andrew S. Cameron, married Susan T. Arnette, a daughter of Mrs. Wesley Mayfield, of Buckhead. He died soon after the war, leaving a widow and one child. She having since died, her son is living with his grandmother, Mrs. Wesley Mayfield. Robert Cameron died during the early part of the war. Alex, the only surviving child, resides near White Oak. He married the second daughter of James W. Younge, by his Crosby-Estes wife. The eldest daughter married Henry Younge, son of John I. Younge, from whom Youngesville took its name.

The second daughter married Dr. Christopher Simonton, a good man and first rate doctor. He moved to Florida, but lived only a short time. She returned to South Carolina with her two children, John and Robert. John, since arriving at manhood, returned to Florida. Tobert is at the old John Simonton homestead, and is one of the most successful planters in that section. Sarah married John Simonton, a brother of Dr. Christopher; he laso moved to Florida, where he soon died . The fourth and youngest daughter married Colonel Lee McAfie, (Colonel LeRoy McAfee, according to his tombstone in Concord Presbyterian Church Cemetery. WTC), of North Carolina. She was one of the prettiest women of the land. She and her husband died early, leaving an infant son, who was reared, and now resides with his grandmother of the old Cameron homestead. Out of this family of eleven children we how have living the old mother, her son Alex, and five grand-children.

Andrew Feaster's second son, Jacob Feaster, married a Kennemore, and died without issue, leaving a good solid estate to be divided between brothers and sisters. One of Andrew Feaster's daughters married E. Wooley, who removed to Edgefield, and thence to Cass, now Barton County, Georgia, where he died, leaving one son, Colonel A. Feaster Wooley. Another daughter married Rundley McShan. They had several children, all of whom removed to the west. The boys Ferdinand and Andy, to Mississippi and Arkansas. One of the daughters, Judith, married Isaac Coleman. She died a few years since in Union County, this state (South Carolina) at the home of one of her daughters, three of whom have married in that county, one to William Tucker; she is not a widow; one to William Jeter, and another to John Jeper. Isaac Coleman still survives. Another daughter of Andrew Feaster married Moses Cockrell. There are only tow children now living, John Feaster Cockrell and Margaret Stone, who married a son of the old Revolutionar soldier before mentioned. She is now 85 years of age. Of the stepson, Adam Cooper all of his descendants moved to Mississippi. His son George, the crack rifle shot of his day, married a Triplet of Chester County. His children all now live in Winston County, Mississippi. Adam Cooper's daughter, Margaret, married Captain William E. Hill, a brother of Simeon Hill, and here the old election, it was called Hill's bok, afterwards Feasterville, and it was then said that as the Hill box goes, so goes the county, and it verified, to the disappointment of many who had run well elsewhere; but Hill's box gave them "Hell"., as the expressed it, and this was so often said that they gave it the name of "Hell's Box." This same Simeon Hill was "one of the old-fashioned, plain, honest" men of the day of whom nothing could be said except in his praise.

  David R. Coleman, the Patriach of the Coleman family in Fairfield, was born in Halifax County, North Carolina, May 19, 1765, and died March 25, 1855. His father, Robert Coleman, married Elizabeth Roe. Robert removed to this country when David was a small boy. His wife gave him 14 children. David Roe, who lived and died on the land first settled by his father when he came here, is still in the passession of descendents of the same name. John R. Coleman moved to Greene County, Alabama. Robert Roe Coleman lived and died where his son, Johathan D. Coleman's widow now lives. Wiley R. Coleman married a Ragsdale, of Chester County, and raised a large family, of whom William Buck was the oldest, and H.J.F.W. Coleman is the youngest. Out of this family only one is now living, H.J.F.W. Coleman, and all except him went west and lived there. They are numbered among the best citizens.

****

THE FEASTERS AND COLEMANS

Installment # 2, from Edrington's History of Fairfield.

Winnsboro, News and Herald, May 21, 1901

Allen R. Coleman married a daughter of Charles Coleman, a cousin; settled, lived and died on Rocky Creek, in Chester County. Here I will mention something out of the general order: Allen R. Coleman's wife presented him with twin daughters, and one of his neighbors, by the name of Gladden, had twin sons, and when these twins grew up, they married. John Gladden married Rebecca, and James Gladden married Betsy Coleman. They both raised large families from whom there is many of the name in both Chester and Fairfield Counties. Griffin R. Coleman moved west and all sight of him has been lost. So, of William R., Sarah and Elizabeth, first and second daughters of Robert Coleman, married and went West. Solomon R. Coleman's children all moved West. He married a distant relative, a daughter of Stephen Coleman; Francis went West, Zerebable died young; Henry Jonathan was the 13th child, next to Ancil, the baby of the family, 14 in all. David Roe Coleman married Edith Beam in 1787 or 1788. Robert F. (Tow-Headed Bob) as he was called, married the eldest daughter of John Feaster and raised two sons and four daughters; the eldest married William Coleman, son of Solomon. The second married Atkins; he died, and she then married Andrew Hancock. They moved to Randolph County, Georgia. The third daughter, the present Mrs. Mayfield, has been married four times; first, to Martin Coleman, and then to James Branon, by whom she had one child. Next she married John Q. Arnette. There were four children by this marriage. Dr. R.C. Arnette is the only surviving child.

Robert Coleman's fourth daughter married Dr. S.W.B. McLurkin, by whom she had three children, and died soon after the war. John J. and Andrew E. Coleman moved West and married there. Both are now dead. Wiley F. Coleman married a Miss Elam, of Chester County (Nancy Elam), and died near Halsellville. His widow moved to Chambers County, Alabama, and died there several years ago, leaving one son, Colonel D.R. Coleman. He is an enterprising farmer of that county. David H. Coleman married a Miss Franklin and lived and died in Green County, Alabama, where he removed soon after his marriage. Wilson H. Coleman also moved to Alabama and married a Miss Johnston there, and died, leaving several children.

Isabelle, first daughter of D.R. Coleman, married Squire Jake Feaster; Elizabeth married Isaac Nolen, moved to Indian Springs, Georgia. After her marriage she rode from her father's to Indian Springs on horse-back, there being no rail-roads in those days, and very poor dirt roads. What would the average woman of today say to taking a horse-back ride of 300 miles or less. She was the mother of ten hildren. She is now living in Smith County, Texas, at the advanced age of 80 years. Sarah, the youngest daughter of D.R. Coleman, died early. The Colemans and Feasters were long lived and splendid types of physical manhood, the average weight about 220, and the most of the Colemans over six feet tall.

Among the early settlers on Beaver Creek and McClures were the Wideners, Beams and Dyes, all of whom moved upon the Chinquapin lands on the line of Chester and Fairfield, where most of their descendants live today. The land they then gave up is now owned by T.M. Lyles, J.C. and T.D. Feaster, and D.P. Crosby, and is considered the best section of Fairfield County.

The Meadors lived on McLines (?) (might mean McClures) Creek. They, the

Hills and the "Cage" and Cullen branch of the Mobley family owned, with the exception of a few small tracts, all that whole country. Dr. W.M. Meador and his boys, Dr. Lem and John Meador, representatives of the last named families, own a portion of the land lying on Beaver Creek and between McClures Creek and the river and north to the Chester line. In this section lived the Nevetts, Jenkins, Sheltons, Newbles, Chapmans, and later, Andrew McConnell, who bought the plantation now owned by J.F.V. Legg from Major William S. Lyles. McConnell was a poor boy, but when he died was the possessor of thousands of acres of land and more than 100 slaves. J.F.V. Legg married his widow and now lives at the old homestead. Further north we had Meredith Poole Meador, who owned the place occupied by Laurens Feaster. Allen (Alben ?) Boulware owned a large tract of land on Broad River. Stephen Crosby lived near the line and owned land in both Chester and Fairfield counties. His oldest son, Thomas, married a Miss Parks, and their son, Charley Crosby now owns nearly all of the land that was his father's and grandfather's. The next son, Coleman Crosby, married a Miss Walker, of Chester County. He was the father of Mrs. Dr. Estes and W.W. Crosby. William Crosby married a Thomas and raised a large family of children. Davis Crosby was quite popular and represented the county in the Legislature. Stephen Crosby married Frances, the oldest daughter of Cornelius Nevitt. He bought from the late Gov. John H. Means the place now owned by his only child, Mrs. D.P. Crosby. It is one of the prettiest places in the up-country. One of old Stephen Crosby's daughter married Charles Douglass, who lived and died near Alston. Richard Crosby, Uncle "Dick", as he was called, married a Conway, and lived to a ripe old age. He and Jacob Stone, his nearest neighbor, were called by the wags of the neighborhood, the "Siamese Twins". They always went to Chester and Columbia together, and returned home with jugs full. They were thrifty and enterprising farmers. It was
    said by the wags that they did not know what Andy Feaster Colvin's boys would have done for wives if "Uncle Dick" had not raised so many pretty girls. All

of the Colvin boys married Crosbys, except one or two.

David Henderson, a brother of old Thomas Henderson, wo lived on Broad River, was considered the ugliest man of his day, and was called "Pretty Dave". He always kept one eye closed and gave as a reason that he did not wish to wear them both out at the same time. There are many quaint sayings and laughable anecdotes told of him which will live here as long as the memory of man liveth, for they are handed down from father to son. He was a man of considerable education for his day and time. Had it not been for whiskey he would have been a useful member of society, but as it was, everybody liked "Pretty Dave". Once when he and his brother, Tom were returning home from Columbia, they met a stranger who looked at Tom in amusement ("Pretty Dave" was lying in the wagon drunk) and said, "You are the ugliest man I ever saw." Tom replied that he would " bet him $5.00 that he could show him an uglier man than he was." The bet was good, and Tom called to his brother, Dave, to look out. The stranger gave him the money, saying that he "had honestly won it."

Old man Simeon Free lived at the head of McClures Creek years ago, but he and all of his children moved to the west. The children of Wiley and Hiram Coleman own all of the Henderson and Free land.

Uncle Tom Williams was a carpenter, millright, etc. He was considered the best man physically speaking in the county. His wife was Dorcas Halsell, whose mother was a Wagener, after whom Fort Wagener was named, that was erected on Beaver Creek. We then had the Gwinns, Weires, Yongues, Mindocks (?) (probably Murdocks). and Macons.

General Ed. Taylor of the "Dark Corner" has been honored by his fellow citizens to every office that he has asked for - first Captain, then Major, then Colonel, and lastly General of the State Militia. He is yet living, and his eyes are as bright, and his step apparently as firm as ever.

John Feaster, son of Andrew Feaster, was the founder of Feasterville Academy, and donated 7½ acres of land to Liberty Church, and 5½ acres to the Academy. Tradition says that John Feaster had the first glass windows in the township. Thomas Coleman lived and died on the premises now occupied by D.R. Feaster, and was the owner of the first brick chimney north of Beaver Creek.

The Chapmans were a numerous and prominent family on McClures Creek. They have all left except Giles Chapman and the widow and children of John Chapman, who owned the old Halsellville property, just beyond the line in Chester County.

Cornelius Nevitt, of whom mention has already been made, had three sons, two of whom are now living. Cornelius now resides at Brooksville, Florida; Joseph K. is living near the old homestead; Jack was killed at Knoxville, Tennessee, in December, 1863; Frances, his eldest daughter, married Stephen Crosby. Precious Ann married Frances H. Ederington, and Brooks married Lanson (?) Withers, then Oliver Waters, then Rev. Mrs. Moore, of North Carolina. Mrs. L.R. Fee is her daughter by her first marriage. Laura, the youngest, married William McWhorter, and live in North Carolina. Charles Waters, her eldest son by her second marriage, married Miss Fannie D. Kerr, daughter of William Kerr, who resides near Shelton, S.C.

On the headwaters of McClures Creek lived old Henry Tynes. Of the "Cage" (Micajah), Cullen, and Isham Mobley families, their name was legion. The Crowders were from North Carolina and were as numerous as the Mobleys, Notly Mobley was the "bully" of the precinct. Big John Cockerel was the "bully" of the White Oak section. He determined he would try manhood with Mobley, but Notly was of a slow and sluggish disposition and had to have coals of fire heaped upon his back before he would move. Cockerel told him he came there to whip him or be whipped. Uncle Isham Mobley could not stand it any longer, and said as much to Notly. When Cockerel turned to him and asked him if he took it up, -- "Yes, by God, I do," was the immediate reply, and at it they went, and John Cockerel went home badly whipped, so he said, and not whipped by the "bully", but by a much smaller man. Such acts as these were not infrequent at that time, and each section had its "bully", and he was honored and respected as such. Robert Mobley, who lives near Woodward, C. C. & A. railroad, is the only one of this branch of the Mobley family living in the country.

Old Bolin Wright came from Virginia and settled about a mile west of Liberty Church, where he died. He was a Revolutionary soldier. The most notable of his children were William Wright, a Baptist preacher of the old school, and Uriah S. Wright, who was noted in his day and time as a "home doctor" and was called by nearly one Dr. Wright. His practice was not confined to Fairfield, but to Chester, Union and Newberry counties, demanded and had his services. He was eccentric, erratic and generous. He was a great fox hunter and what he did not know about fox-hunting was left out of the spelling book.

In 1860 Major T.W. Woodward was a candidate for the Legislature, and stopped with a relative who lived near the "Corner", and on inquiring for the names of those living around, he was told to call on old Wright by all means. "Old Uriah is a fox-hunter, and I am sure you (the Major was a fox-hunter, too) can talk enough about dogs to secure his vote." "Well, give me some points about the pack," said the Major. "Ring Smith is his best strike and Jolly Wright his coldest trailer, and Molly Clowney his swiftest runner." The Major having obtained a description of these dogs, so there would be no difficulty in identifying them, made it convenient to call on old Uriah the next day about dinner time. Old Uriah had just come in from ploughing as the Major rode up to the gate. "This is Dr. Wright, I suppose," said the Major. "That is what Johathan D. and the boys around here calls me." "My name is Woodward and I am a candidate for the

Legislature, and being a young man on my first political legs, I am going around to see and be seen, if not by everybody, certainly by the most prominent and influential citizens of each section." "Git down, you a monstrous likely man, and I'll take you to see Pinkey (his wife), and we will see what she has to say about it." The Major descended and was going into the house to see "Pinkey", the while discussing the crops with old Uriah, when he paused a moment and turning in the direction of some hounds who were lying around in the shade, he said: "Dr. Wright, I am a very peculiar man. I love the ladies dearly, it is true, and yet, I hope, sir, you will pardon my weakness, -- a fine hound dog comes nearer perfection in my eye than any earthly object." "And what do you know about dogs ?" asked old Uriah, turning from the house and following the Major who had gone in the direction of the dogs and was already seated at the foot of a large White oak, with the whole pack around him. He had little difficulty in selecting the dogs of note from the description given him the night before, and after some gereral somment on dogs, he said, " What is the name of this dog?", "Ah ! Ring Smith, you say ? An uncommonly fine dog he seems to be - if there is any truth in signs, he ought to be a mighty strike." "Good strike, did you say? If there were four thousand dogs here, I would bet a million dollars that Ring Smith would open three miles ahead of the best hunter in the bunch, and you might go before a magistrate and swear that is was a fox when he opened," was old Uriah's reply. The Major was now intently examining a large pale black and tan dog which filled the description of Jolly Wright - the coldest dog - feeling his nose and walking around he eyed him intently. "Dr. Wright," said he at last, " I think this one of the most remarkable dogs I have ever seen, just look at that head and feel his nose; I honestly believe this is the coldest dog I have ever seen

"Coldest, did you say? Why he can smell 'em when they have been gone three and four weeks, and if the fur ain't good, he wont open on 'em then." Molly Clowney had been easily recognized and now came in for her turn. "Here ought to be the very apple of your eye," said the Major, "for if I do not know anything about dogs, this is unquestionably the fleetest footed animal I have ever met; tell me now truthfully, can't she out-run anything in these parts?" "Run, did you say? No, she can't run a bit; but there ain't a crow, nor a turkey-buzzard that ever crossed 'the corner' that can hold a light to her a-flying; I have seed her tried against many of 'em. Dinner is about ready and I want Pinkey to meet you." The Major was taken into the house and introduced to Mrs. Wright. "Ain't he likely, Pinkey? Just look at him!" and the old man led him around like a fine horse at a Fair. "And smart! Why he has forgot more than all the other candidates ever knowed. I am sure he must be close kin to old preacher, Billy Woodward, for I heard my daddy say he was the smartest man in the world, and he knowed what he was talking about."

After dinner, the Major having promised to introduce a bill for the benefit of tired dogs, providing that ho fence should be over five rails high, was in the act of leaving when "Old Uriah" called Pinkey to bring his fiddle, saying, "Hold on 'till I play "The Devil's Dream" for you." When he finished his peice, "One good turn deserves another" said the Major, "I'll play a tune for you before I go," and taking up the fiddle , he rendered "Hell Broke Loose in Georgia" , with such spirit and skill that " Old Uriah" jumped up , hugged Pinkey, and cut the pigeon wing all over the room.

It is needless to say that the Major got "Old Uriah's" vote.

****

THE FEASTERS AND COLEMANS

Part # 3

News & Herald, Winnsboro, S.C., Friday, May 24, 1901.

Concluded

David Wright moved off to Jug Tavern, Ga., where he died. William Wright married a daughter of "Cage" Mobley. (Gemimah Mobley). His eldest daughter married Jonathan McLane.

Many of the Hills were known by nick-names, such as "Varment Dick", "Stump Bill", He was a Mobley, "Londee Bill" Hill, "Ly-down", etc. These names were given from certain peculiarities of manner, character, or habits of the man. Where Moses Clowney now lives (and he, Moses, was not an old-timer, is now one of the staunchest citizens of that township,) there lived years ago William Robinson, known as "Boiled Meat Billy." His house was a great resort for those who loved to dance and enjoy themselves. Four of his sons lived here after they were grown, Billy, Willis, Nat and John. The eldest girl married "Guber" Dye; one married John Hancock, and the youngest, Rebecca, married James Gaston, but did not live long. Mr. Gaston then married a daughter of Nathan Parrot. There were then several families of Shirleys. Hatter John or "Lying John" as he was called when he would tell an unaccountable tale, and when doubts were expressed by anyone, he would defend himself by saying, "If it is a lie, Ned Means told it, for he told me." Ned Means was noted for his veracity, and Shirley thought no one would doubt for a moment what he said. "Sugar" John Shirley was just the opposite. He was a miller and shoemaker. His only son was killed in the war. Martin Beam, who is a grandson of his, is now overseer of Feasterville Grange. Mirron Shirley was not bright, and he used to create some amusement by his sing-song way of telling things.

There was a large family of Meltons that lived on Beaver Creek on land now owned by James Turner. I should have mentioned while on the Meadow side of the township, Major William Seymore; he was a leading man, taught singing school when the old Southern Harmony was used. He was major in the militia, and came very near being elected sheriff at the time Emmett Ellison was elected. The Major was second best, and they had one of the very strongest men in the county as a competitor, James Johnston, who was Ordinary just as long as he wished to be. Seymore moved to Randolph County, Alabama, and he is now dead. His wife was a sister of Andrew McConnell.

I omitted at the proper place that Wiley and Henry J. Colemen were both hatters. They made such everlasting hats that it was impossible to wear them out; they had to be thrown away if you wished to rid yourself of them.

Liberty Church was built by those of the Universalist faith, and it was intended as its name indicates, for the use of any and every denomination that was disposed to worship in it. There were others who also contributed to the building besides Universalists.

****

EDERINGTON FAMILY

News & Herald, Winnsboro, S.C., June 10, 1901.

Inasmuch as it is expected that the author of an work should in some degree be known to its readers, either personally or historically, I will endeavor to sketch a short account of my family, As to my ancestry, I have but meager knowledge, such as i recollect from my father's detail and one or two other sources. My Paternal Grandfather, William Ederington, emigrated from Wales in the early settlement of Virginia, and located in what what was afterwards called King George County. He later moved to Stafford County, Virginia. He married a Helm. He, or she, was related to the Metcalfs, Fitz Hughs, and other distinguished families, I have heard my father, as well as my Virginia correspondent, state, whose letters were destroyed with my dwelling in February, 1865, by Sherman's army. Our family furnished two governors for Kentucky, Governors Helm and Metcalf. My grandfather, as I heard my father say, was a member of the House of Burgesses in Virginia, before the Revolutionary War. He rode to South Carolina before the war and surveyed and entered a large tract of land on Rock Creek, Fairfield County, near Broad River, returned to Virginia, and not long afterwards he died. My grandmother removed shortly after his death, with several of her sons and daughters, and settled on this tract in South Carolina. My paternal uncles were all engaged in the Revolutionary War. My father being the youngest, did not engage in it until near its close. I heard him say that he volunteered at the age of sixteen under Captain Charnal Durham and encamped at Four Holes for some time awaiting orders, but soon after Sir Henry Clinton evacuated Charleston, and the corps was disbanded, and the soldiers all left for their homes and were nearly starved before they reached their destination, being afraid to call at any house or allow themselves to be seen, the country through which they had to pass being infested with Tories. Peace was soon after declared. Three of my uncles remained in Virginia until after the war, then moved to South Carolina and settled on the land their father had bought. My uncle, James Ederington, remained only a few years, then moved to Kentucky and many years after to Mississippi, and there died, upwards of a hundred years old. My father was the only one of five brothers who remained on the old homestead, and his grandson, A.L. Ederington, is now living there. My grandmother married a second time during the Revolutionary War, John Davis, from York District, and her oldest daughter married his son, James Davis, who lived near Monticello and died there in 1822. One of my aunts married Ephraim Lyles, son of Ephraim, the first settler, near Lyle's Ford; another aunt married a Furney and another married a McManus. Two of my uncles married in Virginia, the others in this state. My father married Frances Crosswhite, of Newberry County. Her mother was a widow when she left Culpepper County, Virginia, and moved to South Carolina before the Revolutionary War, and settled on Little River in Newberry County. She afterwards married George Griffin, who moved on Broad River near Ashford Ferry, where both died. My father moved to a plantation he bought for my brother, but exchanged his old homestead for it in 1821, and died there on Beaver Creek where his remains are interred. He died in June, 1824, aged sixty years. His small plantation was devised to me after the death of my mother, but she allowed me to sell it and I bought land lf Major Thomas Lyles in 1827 and moved to it, where seh died April, 1829, at the age of sixty-two. My eldest brother, Jesse, married Elizabeth Webb in 1810, an estimable and pious lady. He and she both died in 1863. Their eldest son, William H. Ederington, married in Mississippi, lived in Louisiana, and after the late war, died in Vicksburgh, Mississippi, of yellow fever in 1881. He had been a wealthy planter, had two sons, William and Henry Clay, the latter now living in Fort Worth, Texas, a wealthy banker. James P. Ederington, my brother's second son is also living in Forth Worth, a dealer in landed estate. Henry C. has a family, but James F. never married. Robert J., his third son, died in Texas since the war, and was never married. Harrison E., his fourth son, died in Waco, Texas, about 1858. My brother, John, moved to Kentucky about 1815 and married and died there. My oldest brother, Francis, never married. He died about 1832 in Union County. My oldest sister, Mildred, married William Fant in 1817, and moved to Union County in 1821. He died in 1854, she afterwards lived in Fairfield with her son Dr. F.H. Fant, and died there in 18__ , at the advanced age of ninety-none Her oldest son, O.H.P. Fant, is living in Laurens County, a planter and merchant. He married Liziee Jone, an intelligent and estimable lady. They have five childre alive, two married. The oldest married a wealthy Kentuckian, William Arnold, who is living near Richmond, Kentucky, and has but one child, a promising daughter. The second daughter, Jessie, married Dr. James K. Cilder, of Newberry, an intelligent gentleman and worthy citizen of that town. F.W. Fant, the eldest son, married in Kentucky. He is a lawyer and settled in Spartenburg, S.C. The other two sons, John and Willie, are young, the former in his father's store in Newberry the latter at school in Spartanburg. Dr. F.M.E. Fant was born in Union, S.C., practiced medicine successfully for many years, nd moved in 1867 to the place where I had been burnt out by the Yankees. He still follows his avocation and is besides a good practical planter. Dr. Sam Fant, my sister's third son, practiced medicine several years in Union and Laurens Counties. He moved to Newberry not long after our civil war and was engaged in the drug business until his death, October 8, 1886. In 1871 he married Fannie Lyles, grandaughter of

Major Lyles, of Newberry, an intelligent and estimable lady. They have four promising children, three daughters and a son. My second sister, Elizabeth, married William Vance, of Laurens County, in 1821. He lived and died near Milton. He was industrious, honest and economical, a successful planter and worthy citizen. He died about 1827, leaving nine children, quite a charge for my sister, but she brought them up to labor, and taught them lessons of morality and economy. She moved to Mississippi about the year 1857 and died there a few years afterwards. Her children moved to the west also, except the youngest, Susan, who married Richard Satterwhite, and lived in Newberry, where he died since the war. Carr E. Vance's only daughter, Mrs. Kinard, died in Newberry County in 1885. She was an estimable lady and left only one son, who is at school in Newberry. One of her brothers, L.K., is on the farm she left; the other, Carr E., is living in Texas. My third sister, Sallie, married David Vance, and lived near Milton, Laurens County, and died there in 1832. She left four sons, all are now dead except the oldest, Rosborough, who is living in Rossuer Parish, Louisiana. He never married. Another son, Whitfield, lived and died in the same parish in Louisiana. He married twice. both times Gilmers. He died a few years ago, leaving two children, I believe. The reader will pardon this lenghty mention of my family, I hope, when I assure him that it is not intended so much for the general reader as for my own family and relatives. I will now give a little sketch of my own life.

I was born at my father's old homestead on Rock Creek, in Fairfield County, S.C., February 10, 1803. I was sent ot oldfield school masters, where I learned but little until 1816 when I was sent to James R. Wood, of Newberry County, who was an efficient teacher. I afterwards went to him in Monticello and boarded with him, intending to prepare myself for a teacher of the English branches. I returned home at the end of the year and secured a school worth

$300 and board. I was dissuaded from this enterprise by my friends, Dr. George B Pearson, and Dr. Harris, promising to make an M.D. of me if I would attend Mr Hodge's Latin school about ten months, which I did in 1822, but after I returned I had to attend to my father's farm, which required all of my time and care. I have never had cause to regret not reading and practicing the healing art, but I would have done so had I had the means. As I before stated, my father soon after died, and I moved in 1827 to where I am now living, and engaged in mercantile enterprise with John Smith, as partner, and also ran a farm. John Smith soon after died, He was an estimable, high-toned gentleman from the Wateree settlement; he had formerly been a partner in a store with Major Thomas Lyles. My school and classmates at the Monticello School in 1822, when I took my first course in Latin, were William P. Hutchison, Daniel Dansby and Franklin Davis. The old course of Latin was a tardy one compared with present, and I could almost have gone through with all the classics in ten months in the way Latin is now taught. I studied assidiously, determined to leave my class as soon as possible, which I did, and enter the next highest with stufents who had been some two and some three years in that study, I had as classmates William B. Means, Robert Means, James B. Davis, William K, Davis, and C. De Graffenreid. I recited with these until October and said an extra lesson every morning in Cicero. These together with William M. Nyers, Thomas B. Woodward, James A. Woodword, Cullen Powell, John H. Means, and myself, were boarding with Colonel Jonathan Davis, and our sleeping department was in his old store-house recently fitted up for that purpose. Being the greater part of the time from under the observation of our host and tutor, the reader may well imagine we had a nice time of it, yet the larger number of us were quite studious, This was the first school, strange as it may appear, in which any of us studied geography, although several of the students were fair Greek scholars. Our tutor, Mr. Hodges, a graduate of the South Carolina College, urged us to the importance of geography and wrote to Columbia for Cumming's Geography and Atlas for us, a small book and atlas that would be laughed at by the students of the present day. The maps were not colored; I borrowed a paint box and painted mine, the only colored one in school. Silas H. Heller, afterwards a lawyer and a member of our legislature, was also one of our students, well advanced in the classics. He was from Newberry County and boarded with Mr. Phillip Pearsh, Sr. I must not forget an unpleasant obstacle in our progress, viz: The Bible lessons! We of our own accord received Bible lessons on Sunday evenings. Mr. Hodges after a while neglected to come, and wished to hear the recitations on Monday morning. We rebelled against that and he suspended us for two weeks. At the expiration of the given time, only two returned to his school, S.H. Heller and myself. We came back on our own terms, viz: To drop the Bible lessons, and the five who did not return caused the school to wane and no doubt Mr. Hodges regretted the rash act he adopted. He was a native of Abbeville County, and a contemporary of John C. Calhoun, and I think they were in the South Carolina College together. Mr. Hodges afterwards became an eminent Baptist preacher. I closed my mercantile life in 1840, and bought land on Broad River, and conducted two farms until 1867, when I had become too feeble from old age to manage free labor, and sold both plantations to my nephew, Dr. F.M. Fant, to whom I was in debt. I then taught free schools until 1881 when I was compelled from debility to discontinue. I again ask pardon of the reader for trespassing on his patience in giving the uninteresting history of my long life. It has been a rugged journey to pass through, more so in consequence of ill health in my early and middle life, which I give as an excuse for never having married.

There are no remarkable characteristics in out family to notice; as a general thing we are industrious, honest, candid and inpatient. Some of the descendants of the stock who emigrated from Virginia are physicians and only one lawyer. I have never known one of the family to run for office. When I was a member of the Buckhead troop of cavalry, I was the only exception. A vacancy occured for cornetist, and I found my name posted on the old Buckhead store for that office, without consultation with me. I was elected by a nearly unanimous vote, receiving seventy out of seventy-three. The location of our muster ground was not long after removed and I resigned my commission, the first and last I ever held. It was handed to me by General John H. Means.

****

VARIOUS FAIRFIELD FAMILIES

From The News & Herald, Winnsboro, S.C., June 18, 1901

Rev. James Rogers was for many years Principal of the Monticello Academy in its early existance. He first married a Miss Boyd; they had one son, John. After her death he married Miss Celia Davis, sister of Colonel John Davis; she left no children. Rev. James Rogers was for many years pastor of the Presbyterian Church near Kincaid's bridge, called the Brick Church. He died at White Hall, where Mr. Thomas McGill now lives, about the year 1830. Colonel Hugh Stevenson afterwards lived and died in the same house. Colonel Jonathan Davis was a son of James Davis, who came from York County a short time after the Revolutionary War, and married Miss Mollie Ederington. He became a Baptist preacher about the year 1835. He was a man of liberal education and a rigid disiplinarian in church government. He served Rock Creek, Little River and other churches for many years, even after he became a cripple. He was much devoted to the cause of his Master, and died near Monticello about the year 1860 in full assurance of eternal bliss. I should have mentioned before that Colonel Jonathan Davis married Miss Rebecca Kincaid, a daughter of Captain James Kincaid, one of the pious women I ever knew. While I boarded with them in 1822, she became a cripple for life. She bore her affliction with Christian fortitude and lived many years afterwards. She died at the home of her son-in-law, the Rev. James C. Furman, in Greenville, South Carolina, having been blessed with a long life. No purer woman ever lived. Colonel Jonathan had nine children, six sons and three daughters.

Dr. James B. Davis married a Miss Scott, practiced medicine in Winnsboro, then he became a large planter where he lived near Monticello.

He afterwards spent five years in Turkey in the interest of the Sultan in regard to producing cotton in his Empire. He returned to South Carolina with his family about the year 1845, and died soon after in Fairfield. William K. Davis married a Miss Zimmerman of Darlington County, S.C., and was a planter near Monticello for many years. He afterwards moved to Charleston; he did not remain in the city long before he returned to Fairfield, and died about 1871. He read law in Union County at Mr. John Welshs, but never practiced that profession. He was a very intelligent and well-read man, a devoted husband and father and much beloved by all who knew him. He has a son in Charleston, having his wife's name, Zimmerman. He was colonel of the 5th South Carolina Cavalry in Butler's Brigade, Confederate States Army. W.K. Davis had three other sons and two daughters; Major William J. and Clinn C. Davis, of Louisville, Ky., and Glenn E. Davis, of Charleston, S.C. One of his daughters married Frederick Tupper and the other C.J. Hugenin, both of Charleston. Benjamin F. Davis read and practiced medicine; he graduated at Louisville, Ky., married a Miss Adams, moved to Mississippi and there died. He was regarded as a skillful physician and was a man of more than ordinary calibre. Jonathan Davis moved to California.

Colonel J. Bunyan Davis, fifth son of Col. John Davis, was a brave and efficient officer in our late war. He raised the first company in Fairfield after the State seceded. He was colonel of the 15th Regiment of South Carolina Volunteers and did good service in both state and Virginia. After the war he married a Miss Fuller of the low country, Beaufort, S.C. She died a few years ago, leaving two sons and two daughters, and after her death, Colonel Davis went to Texas a few years, but he returned to his native county and is now engaged in practicing medicine and teaching school near Monticello.

Nathan Davis, a son of Colonel Jon. Davis, is living in Greenville, S.C. Harriet was the oldest daughter of Colonel Davis. She married the Rev. J.C.

Furman and died not long after. The second daughter, Rebecca, died quite young. Mary Glenn Davis was the youngest child; she married her brother-in-law, Rev. James C. Furman. He is now president of Furman University in Greenville, S.C. He and his wife are leading lives of great usefulness to the present and succeeding generations.

I will here make a quotation from Mills' "Statistics of South Carolina," pulbished in 1826, by an act of the Legislature; "Jacob Gibson removed to this State from North Carolina in 1762. He was a minister of the Baptist persuasion and a teacher. .There is no calculating the good which resulted from his labors of love and patience. He was an excellent scholar and a sound, practical preacher. St. Parre esteems the individual who introduces a new species of fruit which may afford support to man, as more useful to his country, and more deserving of its gratitude than the laurelled chieftain of victorious armies. Still more, we might add is to be esteemed he who spends, as Mr. Gibson did, forty years of his,life in devotion to the propagation of the gospel and in sowing the seeds of literature and refinement in a new and scarcely civilized settlement. Mr. Gibson died about the year 1796, but his memory is held in profound veneration by many who remember his exemplary worth."

Believing that but few persons in the county have a history of Fairfield, I again quote from "Mills' Statistics," "Colonel Aromanos Lyles, Col. John Winn, John Gray, Benjemin May, William Strother, John Strother, William Kirkland, Joseph Kirkland, Robert Hancock, John Buchanan, William McMorris, John Cook, Capt. Balar, Capt. Watson and Edward Martin, were among the brave defenders of their country, suffered in her cause, and closed in honor their mortal careers."

General John Pearson was a native of Richland County, he was a well educated and influential gentleman, and at the first alarm flew like a faithful son to his country's standard. He rose to the rank of Major in the militia, was incesant in his exertions to fulfil his duty to the State, and bore the character of a brave and skillful officer. He was chosen colonel of Fairfield (which at the time made but a single regiment), by a popular election shortly after the war, and was afterwards brigadier-general. General Pearson filled many civil offices to the entire satisfaction of the people. He died in 1817." Gen. John Pearson was a member of Congress in Jefferson's administration and received from him a donation ($100) to Monticello Academy, which was named for Jefferson's residence near Charlottesville, Va.

I saw General Pearson at a regimental muster ground when I was a boy, during the War of 1812, I recollect him as he sat upon a large horse in his uniform, as a man of low, well formed stature, of dark complexion. I know his sons, Philip and John; the latter married first my cousin Nancy Furney. They had several children. After planting on Beaver Creek several years, he moved to Alabama about the year 1830. This was after he had married his second wife, Sallie Hill, who lived a few miles above old Buckhead. Philip moved to Union County where he died. Gen. Peawson's daughter, Martha, married James Rush about the year 1825, who kept a hotel in "Cotton Town" first, and then lower down in Columbia, S.C. One daughter, _____, married Richard O'Neal, Sr., well known as a merchant and cotton buyer in Columbia, for more than fifty years. Gen. Pearson's other daughters married the following named gentlemen: James Elkin, Mr. McKerny, Thompson Mayo, and another, Benjamin V. Lakin. James Elkin had several children. David John Ford's daughter. I knew but one of his children, Bayliss, who died not long since, near Ridgeway; he was a member at or time of the State Legislature. Rev. William Elkin, a Baptist minister, is now living at Walhalla. One of James Elkin's daughters married her soucin Major Elliott Elkins. Both are dead. They left several children. David E. Elkins is a merchant at Alston. J. Bunyan Elkins is living in Greenville, S.C.

Grace Pearson married Benjamin V. Lakin, an intelligent and useful citizen from Faquier County, Virginia. He died some years since, a pious and consistant member of the Baptist Church. His widow died a few years ago at the advanced age of ninrty-nine years. She also was a good Baptist.

In this connection I will mention Major Henry W. Parr, a nephew of B.V. Lakin, from the same State and County. He died at the old homestead of Gen. John Pearson. This house was built during the Revolutionary War, or just after.

The eldest daughter of Gen. Pearson married Dr. Smith of Columbia, who was a half brother of B.V. Lakin. They left several children, two of them were physicians.

I again quote from "Mills' Statistics", "James Kincaid was a native of Ireland. In the Revolution he took that 'better part' which so many others, natives and foreighers, thought at the time was a hazardous enterprise, and would in the end be stigmatized and punished as a rebellion. Mr. Kincaid commanded a troop of cavalry at the Battle of Eutaw, in which affair he greatly distinguished himself. He was, after the return of better times, a member from Fairfield, for many years, of the State Legislature. He was the first purchaser of cotton in the up-country and did more than any other individual to enrich it by giving encouragement to the production of that great staple of South Carolina. Captain Kincaid died of a malignant fever in Charleston in 1800." History awards the invention of the cotton gin to Whitney, but it seems wrongfully, from the following paragraph published in the Columbia Register during the New Orleans Exposition:

"Among the South Carolina exibits at New Orleans will be the original letters patent of parchment, signed by G. Washington, President, and granted to H. Holmes, of South Carolina, for a cotton gin. A letter accompanies the patent written by Mr. George H. McMaster, of Winnsboro, S.C., which expressed the belief that Whitney filched the invention from Holmes, and that 'James Kincaid, a soldier of the Revolution, being told by his friend, Holmes, who lived near Hamburg, in this State, that he had invented a cotton gin, agreed to take the gin and try it at his mill, which was located in the western part of Fairfield County. He did so, and while the mill was closed for a few hours, in the absence of Kincaid, a young man rode to the house and requested of Mrs. Kincaid permission to examine the mill. She, forgetting the injunction of her husband not to permit anyone to enter the mill during his absence, gave the key to the young man, who returned it in a short time and rode off."

Mr. Kincaid subsequently learned that the young man was Whitney, and this is believed by Kincaid's descendants, who still own the mill site. The old, original cotton gin was burned, along with the mill, at the time of Sherman's destructive march through the State. Dr. William Cloud, who married a daughter of Holmes, preserved the parchments. Accepting it as true that the cotton gin was the invention of a South Carolinian, it will be seen that she has led all the States in everything connected with the great southern staple. She invented the cotton gin, and her legislature was the first to pay a royalty for its use. The only improvement on the gin saw has recently been patented by a South Carolinian, and the "Cotton Harvester" is a South Carolina invention."

I have heard my father say that the first cotton/gin he ever saw was owned by Capt. James Kincaid and propelled by waterpower. There were no cotton presses then, nor for many years afterward. What little there was produced was, after being ginned, packed in round bales. The process was this: A circular hole was made in the gin house floor, the bagging sewed together, making a round bale about six feet long, and two and a half in diameter. This bag was confined at the top around the circular hole, into which the cotton was put from above in small quanities at a time, and trodden down by a heavy man, having a maul, or often a crowbar, to pack it with. Another person was on the ground below. whose office it was to keep the bag wet outside by means of a tub of water and a broom. The bales weighed from two hundred and fifty to three hundred.

The first cotton presses, (then called screws) were used about the year 1810 or 1812. The common weight of a bale of cotton prior to 1828 was three hundred pounds.

Captain James Kincaid had several daughters and one son. Daniel McMahon, of Pinckneyville, I think, married the oldest daughter. I knew their sons, James, Daniel and John. James went to the West. Daniel remained in Union for many years. He practiced medicine and planted there. John, after graduating in medicine, practiced his profession for a few years, and turned his attention to planting. He married Miss Sue Heynesworth, fo Sumter, in 1858, and died at his home near Ashford's Ferry in 1865 of typhoid fever. His widow, two daughters and son, are now living in Columbia. His son, John, graduated this year at the South Carolina University with high honors. One of Capt. Kincaid's daughters married Dr. Ervin, of Greenville, another Col. Hill, of Alabama, one a Mr. Harris, of Mississippi, and , I think, one married Colonel John Glenn, of Newberry County. A Mr. Pope, of Edgefield, also married a daughter of Capt. Kincaid. She did not live long and left one son, James Pope. Another daughter, Nancy, married Colonel Alexander B. Hall, of York County. They lived near my father's. Colonel Hill was a tailor, the only one in the vicinity. He was fond of a joke and kept a tavern on the Chester and Winnsboro road. They had two daughters, Mary, the older, died in the bloom of youth, a beautiful girl, Jane, the other daughter, married James B. Mobley, in 1821 and died soon after. Colonel William Kincaid, the only son, married a Miss Calmus of .... He lived at his father's homestead and was an extensive and ... (part of ms missing) He built a large brick barn and stables, reared his horses, mules, cattle, hogs, and sheep. He owned a mill propelled by water power, and ground grain as well as sawed lumber. He was noted for his industrious and economical habits. He kept a store in which hemsold general merchandise. He bought cotton in the seed and ginned. He was the owner of a landed estate and many slaves. He commanded a company of militia during the War of 1812. He died in Charleston in the year 1835. His widow lived many years afterwards and proved to be an efficient manager of her planting interests. Colonel Kincaid left four sons and many daughters. The eldest, Elizabeth, married Mr. Edward Anderson, of Charleston, a nephew of John Kirkpatrick, factor and commission merchant. He died not long after their union and she never married again. She was/a very intellectual and estimable lady, and died a few years ago, leaving an only son, Thomas. He managed her farm and mill many years, and is at present an agent on the Columbia Canal. Nancy Kincaid married a Mr. Hastings. She died in 1886, leaving no children. One daughter of Capt. Kincaid married a Mr. Armstrong, who died not long after, leaving a son and daughter.

****

SOME PROMINENT FAIRFIELD FAMILIES.

News & Herald, Winnsboro, S.C. Friday, July 5, 1901

The Kirklands were Scotch, and lived on Cedar Creek, Fairfield County. They were gallant supporters of the cause of American Independence. This anecdote is related: "Once old Mr. Kirkland (grandfather of Colonel William J. Alston and his sister, Mrs. Dr. Pearson) and another male member of his family , probably a son, were on a visit to their home during the war. A party of Tories found it out and undertook to capture them. They heard of it and left to rejoin their command. When they arrived at some stream, they had to cross, it was night and they found the enemy encamped on the other side. They setermined to make a dash for it and surprise them. Knowing the clatter of their horses' feet on the bridge would sound as though there were more than two riders, they put spurs to their horses and calling to some imaginary followers to come on, they charged the enemy's camp and carried it. The latter taking to their heels."

Although it was a large family, there is not one left of the name in Fairfield.

Frances Kirkland, one of the daughters, was born August 18, 1777. She married James Alston; one of their children was Elizabeth M. Alston, who married Dr. George E. Pearson on December 29, 1814. Mrs. Pearson was a woman of marked characteristics, being generous and charitable to an unusual degree. She was born on Cedar Creek in Fairfield, on December 9, 1799.

William Kirkland , a grandson of Joseph Kirkland, a prominent physician years ago in Charleston, died in Virginia in June 1862 , from wounds received in battle; he was the last of the name of this family of Kirklands, except his own young children. He was a member of the Charleston Light Dragoons, and was a rice planter of Colleton District. He married a daughter of Judge Withers; I think he still lives in Camden, S.C.

Col. William J. Alston, son of James Alston and Frances Kirkland, was born July 21, 1802. He was a man of wealth, education and intelligence, and was a member of the Legislature from this county from 1840 to 1846. When a vacancy occured in the Seccession Convention, caused by the death of John Buchanan and William S. Lyles, members of that body from this county, he and William R. Robertson were elected to fill the vacancies.

Col. Alston had built a fine large house a short time before the Civil War; Sherman's "fleur de chevalerie" burnt it, although his family and other ladies were in it when fired. Mrs. Alston and her little children took refuge in another house on the place and were again driven forth and that house burned. I suppose those who applied the torch soothed their consciences if not too scared to feel, by saying that they were turning women and children out of doors in winter, "to preserve the Union !" The peculiar atrocities perpertrated on this place and that of Mrs. William S. Lyles were ascribed to the fact that the owners had been members of the Secession Convention.

Colonel Alston died on the 4th of July 1868. He had a presentment of his death, and the message came not unexpected. He had been for years a consistant member of the Methodist Episcopal Church, South, and contributed largely to the building of the church in Monticello. He was twice married; his first wife was Miss Mariana Brown, of John's Island, S.C. and their children were; James Henry, William Samuel, Kirkland and Marian Kennan. James Henry died when a child and Marian Kennan, than whom no braver, more lovable young man ever lived, fell mortally wounded at the battle of

South Mountain, Maryland, September, 1862. Nothing more was ever learned of his fate. Colonel W. S. Alston is the only surviving child of this marriage. He married Miss Edith Matthews of John's Island ; they had two children. both of whom are now dead. Colonel and Mrs. Alston moved to North Carolina about fifteen years ago and now live in Hendersonville.

Colonel William J. Alston married again in 1852 Miss Susan P. Cook, the beautiful and affable daughter of the late General Philip Cook. They had three children; Philip Cook, a most estimable youth , who died of Consumption in 1874; Frances Kirkland, a girl of an unusually lovely character; firm, yet gentle and patient, who died June 10, 1876 at the home of her guardian, Major T.W. Woodward, endeared by her noble traits to all who knew her.

Joseph Kirkland Alston, the only surviving child of this marriage, was last year admitted to the bar of South Carolina, and is now engaged in the practice of law in Columbia. Mrs. Susan Alston died in 1870 in Spartanburg, whither she had gone to educate her three children.

John Alston, Sr., grandfather of Colonel William J. Alston and Mrs. Pearso, belonged to an English family, though when he came to this country, he came from Scotland. He was a graduate of Glascow University, and by profession a civil engineer. His commission from the crown as engineer was destroyed in the house of Colonel William J. Alston, which was burned by Sherman's vandals in February 1865. He was married to Mary Boyd April 7, 1768. They had quite a large family. The names of the children were; Charnel, Margaret, Mary, James, David, Jane, Agnes, Anne, John, and several who died in infancy. Samuel was born December 14, 1769 and died July 30, 1834. He was quite a prominent man in the district and lived and died in the house in which he was born, on Cedar Creek. This old brick house was destroyed by Sherman in 1865.

David Alston married and left three sons, John, who was for a time principal of the Mount Zion College, and who died in Winnsboro, in 1859; William L., who perished with Fanning's men March 27, 1846, in the fort Goliad, Texas. James died in 1848. The two last never married.

James Alston married Frances Kirkland ; they had but two children: Elizabeth M., who married Dr. G.B. Pearson; and Colonel William J. Alston. James Alston was a man of remarkable firmness of character and strength of mind. He amassed a large property and was ever noted for his charity and general nobility of disposition. He died in 1841, universally respected.

Anne Alston, daughter of John Alston and Mary Boyd, married James Owens and became the mother of Alston, Samuel, James, William, Jesse and Mary Owens. She was a noble hearted woman and lived to an old age. Her children all had sterling qualities of head and heart.

Alston Owens was a young man of great promise, but he died in early life, soon after having graduated in law with distinction.

Samuel H. Owens studied medicine and graduated at the Charleston Medical College. He did not practice his profession long, but became a planter. He served in our State Legislature from 1846 to 1848, in company with E.G. Palmer, J.R. Aiken and W.W. Boyce, being at the head of the ticket in the election. He first married Miss Alice Heath, by whom he has one daughter living, Mrs. J.S. Lewis, of Marion County, Florida. He married a second time in 1847, Miss Mary A. Dantzler, of Orangeburg, a sister of Colin Olin M. Dantzler. There were two children by this marriage, one daughter, now Mrs. J.W. Waldo, and one son, Albert W. Owens, who studied law and has located in Jacksonville, Fla. He is at present State Solicitor in the circuit courts. Colonel Samuel H. Owens and his brother, William, moved to Marion County, Florida, about the year 1854, and were at one time largely engaged in cotton planting. Colonel Owens was elected to the senate (state) and preserved the high stand in his adopted he held in that of his nativity. He died December 13, 1886.

Mr. James B. Owens first moved to Mississippi. He afterwards joined his brothers in Florida , and was a member of the Confederate Congress from that State. He was at one time a preacher of the gospel, but had to desist from using his voice in that way on account of bronchial troubles. He was twice married and is now living in the midst of a large and cultured family. He and his brother Samuel are engaged successfully in orange culture and truck farming.

General William A. Owens was a noble , generous man. He died at his home in Marion County, Florida, in 1867, of congestive chills , universally lamented. His widow, two daughters and a son, still live in the beautiful home he made for them. Not many miles distant from Orange Lake. Jesse, the youngest son of Anne and James Owens, Sr., graduated at the South Carolina College and was at the head of the ticket for representative to the legislature in 1848, having 1,132 votes. He married Miss Sallie S. Woodward, and died in a few years , leaving one little daughter and one son. The daughter, Jessie, married Major Booteu, of Georgia. She was a woman of fine mind and contributed articles to several newspapers. She died a few years ago , leaving three daughters and two sons.

The son, James Owens, while on a visit to his uncle's , enlisted in the 6th Florida battalion, during our late civil war , and after being in active service under General Finnegan, he went with his command to Virginia. The color bearer having been shot down, he gallantly took up the flag and was instantly killed, at the battle of Cold Harbor, Virginia, June 1, 1864, not yet being eighteen years old. His mortal remains are interred at the Presbyterian churchyard in Winnsboro, S.C. and his grave receives its annual tribute of flowers on Memorial day with the other heroes of the Lost Cause.

Mary, the only daughter of Anne and James Owens, Sr., married Dr. William Smart. They moved to Mississippi, where she died about 1850. She left one child who married Captain Tully S. Gibson, of Sunflower County, Mississippi. She refuged with her cousin, Major T.W. Woodward, in Fairfield, S.C., during the war and on returning home at its close, she and both of her little sons were drowned by the sinking of the boat in the Yazoo River. She was a lovely, warmhearted young woman, and her death caused great grief to her gallant husband and stricken father.

Margaret Alston married Samuel McKinstry. I think they had three children who lived to be grown. John McKinstry, who moved to Alachua County, Florida; Thomas McKinstry, who was a good farmer and was one of the representatives in the legislature from Fairfield during the war, and Nancy, who married Capt. Billy Broom. Mr. Thomas McKinstry died a few years ago. He was a man of sound judgement, sterling integrity, and strong religious faith. He had one promising young son, Sergt. W.D. McKinstry, killed at Spottsylvania Court House, Virginia, May 12, 1864 during the civil war. Three children survive him, Dr. Tom McKinstry and two married daughters, Mrs. Gibson and Mrs. Cauthan.

During the early lives of the Owens young men, athletics, sports-wrestling, etc., were much practiced. William and Sam and Jesse were powerful men and were continually testing their strength with other young men. One family, conspicuous for their size and strength, were Robert, Henderson, Dave and Frank Hughes, who were pretty well matched with the Owens. In Winnsboro at that time were a number of young lawyers, James Rutland, E.C. Palmer, William M. Bratton, John M. Buchanan, W.W. Boyce, and J.B. McCants, They had great enjoyment putting on each other practical jokes, No one would have a joke put on him without having his turn. Rutland would come back at Dr. Sam Owens by getting in a crowd and telling the following: After Sam graduated in medicine and returned home, the first time he came into town, being a wealthy young gentleman, he was dressed in top of fashion suit - fine beaver, blue broadcloth, lizzard-tail coat, with bright flat brass buttons, buff vest and elegant pants. Having just graduated, he invited all his friends to take a drink with him at Aiken's store. The liquors were kept at the north end of the store on a raised platform, there being a cellar below, where the liquors were stored. Owens walked back and there being a crowd, he stepped behind the counter and aided Rutland, who was one of the clerks at that time, to hand out the decanters. While this was going on, Mr. David Aiken looked out of the counting room, which was at the south end of the store, and said to his son, Joe, who was also a clerk, "Joseph, who is that yonder behind the counter with Jim Rutland ?". Joe replied, "Sam Owens." Mr. Aiken said, "Joseph, go there and watch him." Joe replied, "Wht, Pa., that is sam Owens." "Well, Joseph, I dont care a damn who he is; just go there and watch him, I tell you. I have seen many a fellow dressed just as fine as he is that would steal. You just watch him." This story would always bring the laugh on Owens, who would have to rack his brain to some back on Rutland.

General William Owens was kind hearted and was very popular, but was irascible and sometimes a little overbearing and generally used vigorous language intermixed with profane expletives. On one occasion he had a difficulty with a Mr. Watt from Little River neighborhood. They were both in town on a public day. Owens being on the pavement and Watt in the hotel piazza, Owens cursed him furiously. Watt did not reply but walked up and down the piazza. After a while John Cockrell, who was about a 200 pounder, as were also Owens and Watt, walked up and said, "Well, Watt, I suppose the timber wont make it." "Yes it will," said Watt, "if I can have fair play."

"I'll see to that," said Cockrell, pulling off his coat. Watt and Owens pulled theirs off and went at it. Bystanders said the blows were like mules kicking. After a long struggle it resulted in a drawn battle, to the surprise of all, for Watt had no reputation of being a fighter, and Owens had.

In the friendly tussels of the Owens', they were very rough sometimes. Once when General John Bratton was quite a young man, he was riding in a spring wagon when William Owens on a hunt or a fish, and without warning, Owens tried to throw him out of the wagon, but Bratton got the turn on him, and pitched him headlong out.

****

THE WOODWARD FAMILY

News & Herald, Winnsboro, S.C. July 9, 1902

John Woodward, oldest son of the "Regulator", resided on the "Anvil Rock" plantation where he also died and is buried. He was a man of great worth and sterling integrity, well known and generally respected. At the death of his father, he raised a sompany and went promptly into service. He married Esther, daughter of Daniel McDonald, and raised three sons, Major John, Col. William T., and Osmund, and three daughters, Sallie, Cynthia and Mary Collins. Major John Woodward I did not know personally. He resided on the Wateree side of the District, and married Patie Axum. He was a successful planter and most worthy citizen. His second wife was Alice Williamson, by whom he had one daughter, Esther, who married Matthias (?) Clarke. After his death, she moved to Louisiana. The children by his first wife were two daughters, Cynthia, who married Dr. Caleb Clarke; Sallie, who married William S. Lyles, and had three sons, as follows: Thomas, the youngest, I did not know. He moved to Mississippi. I knew his son, Major John J. Woodward, who married Rebecca, daughter of P.E. Pearson, a lawyer of Winnsboro. They moved to Alabama, near Talladega. I visited Major Woodward in Talledega in 1856. He was then engaged in the practice of law and was solicitor. He afterwards became judge of the circuit in which he lived. He was killed in the late war while in command of his regiment, the 10th Alabama. He was brave, generous, affable, and altogether the old type of a Caorlina gentleman, He is buried at the Presbyterian Church, Winnsboro.

     Dr. Osmund Woodward, his brother, was regarded as quite a skillful physician. His health was never vigorous. He married Eliza, daughter of David Aiken, of Winnsboro, and died about 1850. while not more than thirty years old. His consort is a most estimable lady, and I think is yet living in Abbeville.

     Col. William T. Woodward lived at his old homestead, three and a half miles below Winnsboro, and died there the 15th of August 1842. He was a man of brilliant talents and a ripe scholar. He married, first, Jane. daughter of Reuben Starke, of Longtown. She was an accomplished woman and is said th have owned the first piano introduced in the district. His second wife was Harriet Smart, noted as one of the handsomest women of them day. Her mother was a McLemore. His third wife was a Mrs. Henry, a sister of Chancellor Job Johnstone. There were no children except by the second wife. She had three; Mary Ann Collins, Major Thomas W. and Esther. Mary died before she was grown. Major Thomas W. was senator from Fairfield, married Cornelia M. Dentzler, of Orangeburg, a sister of Col. Olin W. Dantzler, on the 15th of February 1854. She had no children, but acted well the mother's part to four of her brother's sons, orphaned by the war, also to Fannie K., daughter of the late Colonel William Alston. She was warm hearted, unselfish, candid and kind. In her the poor always found a friend. She died August 21, 1878. Major Woodward then married Rebecca V. Lyles, a daughter of Captain Thomas M. Lyles. Major Woodward is well known, not only in his county, but throughout the State. He was major of the 6th S.C. Regiment in the late war, and has filled many important offices in which he has given evidence of integrity, efficiency and devotion to the good of State and county. Bold and unswerving in purpose, and inheriting more of the traits of the "Regulator" than any of his descendants. He was of incalculable service during the dark days of reconstruction, and seemed to have adopted Davy Crockett's motto, "Be sure you are right, then go ahead." Esther, the youngest child, married Edward, oldest son of Colonel John Woodward, of Talladega, Alabama. They reside now in Waco, Texas, and have three children; Mary (now Mrs. Carter), William T., and Hattie.

Sallie, eldest daughter of John Woodward, Sr., married General William Strother, who had but one child, a son, Dargan, who first married a Miss Pope, of Newberry. They had three daughters and a son, all of whom are now dead. The son entered promptly in the service of his country, and was killed in one of the battles in the West. After the death of his first wife, Captain Dargan Strother married Miss Kate Dunovant of Chester, and a few years after, moved to Louisiana and then to Texas, and died a few years ago in Waco. General William Strother was a highly respected gentleman and an excellant farmer, a kind neighbor and husband and the ideal of an old South Carolina gentleman. He allowed his name to be placed in nomination for congress in 1821. His antagonist was the formidable Starling Tucker, of Laurens County. The congressional district to which they belonged then consisted of Fairfield, Newberry, and Laurens. Tucker was returned by a small majority. General Strother died where he had lived for many years, not far from Winnsboro, about the year 1830, loved by all who knew him. At his own expense he repaired Mount Zion College and built tenement houses on the college ground. He was a benefactor to mankind. Mary Collins Woodward, daughter of John Woodward, Sr., married Major Thomas Lyles. She was a most amiable lady, a good mother, a devoted wife, and a kind neighbor, especially to the poor in sickness. I lived a near neighbor to her for many years and I never knew a purer or more consistant Christian. She was for a long time a member of Rock Creek Baptist Church. She bore her last affliction with much fortitude, and died in 1855 in full hope of a blessed immortality. Osmund, the youngest son of John Woodward, Sr., lived on the Anvil Rock plantation, and afterwards, in Winnsboro. He married Martha Williamson, a daughter of Roland Williamson, who resided on the place known now as Simpson's Turnout, where old Billy Simpson afterwards lived and died. He raised no sons, although he had several. The daughters were Jemima, who married John R. Harrison, of Longtown; Sallie Strother, who married Jesse Owens, and after his death, Dr. John Cock, of Marshallville, Ga.; Lucy, who married Thomas Heath, then David Mobley, then Keller; Rebecca, the wife of Dr. B.A. Buchanan, and Regina, who married Christopher Gadsden. He was a large and successful planter, represented the District in the legislature and was universally beloved and respected by all who knew him. He was a consistent member of the Blackstock Baptist Church, near to Furmans (?) Institute. No truer friend to the poor ever lived. He died during the war, and his remains lie in an unmarked grave in the family burial ground near Simpson's Turnout.

****

1790 CENSUS OF FAIRFIELD COUNTY, SOUTH CAROLINA

This record shows the name of the Head of each family in this county, with the number of free white people living in each house. The names in this record do not appear in the index.

Andrews, David............ 5
Andrews, James............ 9
Andrews, John............. 6
Austin, William........... 9
Andrews, Owen............. 6
Andrews, Edward........... 7
Alston, Samuel............ 9
Arledge, Amos............. 7
Arledge, Joseph........... 7
Andrews, James............ 6
Arledge, Clements......... 9
Arnat, Samuel............. 8
Austin, James............10
Ashford, George........... 2
Amons, Thomas............. 9
Adams, Robert............. 7
Aiken, Walter............. 4
Arnat, James.............11
Arthur, James............. 3
Alsup, William...........10
Aiken, Sarah.............. 7
Adam, William............. 4
Adam, Richard............. 3
Aperson, John............. 1
Adair, Belithe............ 8
Arick, Frederick.......... 2
Ashley, Joseph............ 3
Aitcheson, Mary........... 6
Aitheson, John............ 5
Addison, Thomas........... 8
Addison, Christopher...... 6
Alcorn, James............. 5
Armstrong, John........... 4
Ayers, Moses.............. 4
Ashford, George........... 1
Abbot, John............... 2
Arledge, Isaac............ 2
Arledge, Moses............ 1
Anthony, Paul............. 1
Andrews, Solomon.........10

Bell, William............. 3
Boyd, Andrew.............. 5
Bell, John................ 2
Boyd, William............. 5
Brown, James.............11
Brown, Patrick............ 2
Boyd, Robert.............. 6
Busby, Mark..............11
Bennit, Mrs............... 1
Bell, John, Jr............ 4
Briant, John.............. 3
Bishop, Patrick........... 5
Boulware, Muscoe.......... 6

Burks, James.............. 4
Blake, Fanny.............. 4
Blair, Adam............... 9
Brice, William............ 3
Brady, Robert............. 2
Bolard, Robert............ 6
Baird, William............ 7
Bowls, James.............. 6
Brice, John............... 4
Boney, Jacob.............. 8
Brunt, John............... 8
Brown, Jesse.............. 8
Badger, Joshua............ 7
Brewenton, Thomas......... 4
Brown, Mary............... 6
Brunt, Alex............... 8
Boyd, Samuel.............. 7
Brown, John............... 2
Bennet, Mrs............... 2
Burns, John..............10
Burk, Elizabeth........... 5
Boner, John..............10
Boyd, David............... 5
Burns, John............... 7
Bishop, John.............. 8
Brown, John............... 5
Burns, William............ 8
Burns, Thomas............. 8
Brady, Thomas............. 3
Barker, Samuel............ 5
Barker, Jacob............. 6
Barker, Jacob, Jr......... 7
Barker, Benjamin.......... 4
Brashear, Brasil.......... 7
Beam, Jesse............... 5
Beam, Albert.............. 9
Bell, George.............. 5
Betho, Peter.............. 5
Broom, William............ 9
Blanton, John............. 9
Brewbaker, Jacob.......... 6
Bradford, Thomas.......... 3
Beesly, Margaret.......... 2
Beesly, George............ 5
Beaty, Samuel............. 5
Butler, James............. 9
Butler, Ephraim........... 5
Blake, John............... 2
Blake, Archibald.......... 1
Berry, William............ 3
Briant, William........... 3
Brown, George............. 2
Bradly, William........... 7

Bethany, Jacob............ 8
Bishop, Joseph............ 8
Bishop, Drury............10
Boltner, Lewis............ 6
Buchanan, John............ 2
Branon, Hugh.............. 7
Bradley, Sherard.......... 3
Bradley, John............. 1
Bradley, William.......... 1
Burn, Dennis, Jr.......... 5
Belton, Jonathan.......... 4
Bugs, Frederick........... 6
Bradley, Lewis............ 1
Bishop, Luke.............. 1
Briant, William........... 6
Bishop, James............. 7
Bradford, John............ 6
Boyd, Benjamin............ 9
Blake, Archelaus.......... 5
Briant, John.............. 6
Brazeal, William.......... 4
Blake, John............... 2
Bird, Michael............. 6
Briant, Edward............ 1
Boylstone, Wuldrim........ 2
Boyleston, George......... 2
Burns, Dennis............. 3
Brown, Stephen............ 4
Bradley, John............. 1
Bradley, William.......... 2

Currey, Dudley...........10
Coon, George.............. 4
Cameron, James............ 4
Cameron, Simon............ 6
Cameron, James............ 3
Campbell, Mary............ 3
Cardin, Jane.............. 6
Craig, James.............. 7
Cameron, Jane............. 3
Currey, Jacon............. 7
Curry, Peter.............. 6
Craig, William............ 7
Chappell, John............ 1
Cameron, Thomas, Jr....... 2
Cameron, Thomas, Sr....... 6
Cameron, James............ 4
Cook, Burril.............. 3
Cook, John...............12
Cambell, David............ 4
Curry, Stafford..........11
Cathcart, Joseph.......... 9
Colvill, William.......... 7
Cameron, Joseph........... 4

Cason, Labon............. 1
Cason, Canon............. 5
Caldwell, John........... 5
Caldwell, Thomas......... 2
Cockrell, Moses.......... 9
Colwell, Samuel.......... 4.
Cockral, Moses........... 6
Cockral, Jeremiah........ 3
Clayton, Jane............ 4
Cooper, Peter............ 4
Coleman, Robert.......... 2
Coleman, Thomas.......... 6
Con, Francis............. 7
Cockral, Thomas.......... 4
Cannamore, George........ 7
Coleman, Robert, Sr......10
Chapman, William......... 9
Coleman, William.........10
Coleman, David........... 4
Cork, John...............10
Cameron, Andrew.......... 5
Colaman, Emily........... 6
Curry, Samuel............ 6
Cason, William........... 7
Cato, William............ 6
Carter, John............. 6
Cockran, Daniel.......... 7
Craig, Catherine......... 7
Crim, Peter.............. 8
Cloud, Joseph............ 6
Cooper, Adam............. 7
Carrell, Edward.......... 3
Calvert, Edward.......... 5
Compte, John............. 5
Craig, John.............. 7
Calvit, Peter............ 8
Calvit, John............. 4
Crosslin, John........... 5
Crabb, Daniel............ 6
Crosslin, Samuel......... 4
Cole, Widow.............. 6
Cloud, William........... 5
Cloud, Joseph............ 6
Clayton, John............ 1
Crim, Peter.............. 8
Cason, Whitis............ 3
Charleston, Widow........ 5
Campbell, Isaac.......... 4
Crumpton, Henry.......... 6

Dabney, John............. 5
Daniel, William..........14
Daniel, James............ 3
Dodds, James............. 4
Dodds, John.............. 6
Dunn, Jesse.............. 5
Dunlap, John............. 3
Dodds, Joseph............ 2
Dodds, Thomas............ 2
Davidson, Joseph......... 2
Duncan, Robert........... 2
Dunklin, Sarah........... 5
Dickey, John............. 9

Dodds, Samuel............ 1
Dillard, James........... 9
Dillard, Edmond.......... 2
Doughty, David........... 6
Dye, John................ 8
Day, Edward.............. 7.
Day, Hinson.............. 6
Day, Bollard............. 1
Dove, Benjamin........... 5
Dove, Benjamin, Jr....... 9
Duggins, Leander......... 3
Dunn, William............10
Dortch, John............. 5
Day, Chirtopher.......... 3
Dungan, Jonathan......... 7
Durphy, Prudence......... 8.
Derham, Charnell......... 7.
Dent, William............ 4
Duggans, Richard.........10
Dunn, Joel............... 9
Dilashmate, Celia........ 6
Duke, Moses.............. 7
Dunn, David.............. 7
Duke, Thomas............. 9
Duke, Robert............. 4
Duke, Samuel.............11
Dortch, William.......... 8.
Day, Hinson.............. 6
Dansbie, Mrs............. 6.
Davis, Edmund............ 4
Dyrand, George........... 4
Davies, Levi............. 2
Dickason, James.......... 7
Dozier, John............. 5
Dugins, John............. 1
Dyggins, William......... 3
Dawkins, Richard......... 9
Dawkins, Jesse........... 1
Davies, Adams............ 3
Dawkins, Thomas.......... 6.
Derham, Joshia........... 7.
Davies, James............ 7.
Day, Matthews............ 8

Elliott, James........... 2
Ellison, John............ 6
Elliot, John............. 7
Ellison, Robert.......... 9
Evans, David............. 6
Elliot, John............. 7
Ellison, Robert.......... 9
Evans, David............. 6
Elliot, John............. 7
Elliot, John, Jr......... 5
Ewing, Robert............ 4
Ewing, William........... 3
Elders, John............. 5
Ederington, Christopher..10
Ederington, James........ 7
Ephart, Adam............. 5
Evans, R. Davis.......... 1
Ellison, Robert.......... 9

Elkin, John.............. 7
Elliott, John............10
Elkin, Johnson........... 8

Fort, Jesse.............. 5
Folley, John............. 5
Flowers, John............ 6
Friday, John............. 7
Frazier, Andrew.......... 3
Fletcher, Thomas......... 5
Freeman, Rebecca......... 8
Frazier, William......... 7
Foy, Timothy............. 2.
Foy, George.............. 3.
Ford, Hezekiah........... 4.
Ford, Gardner............ 6.
Fellows, Matthias........ 2.
Frazier, Elizabeth....... 3
Frazier, Mary............ 8'
Freeman, Harriss......... 7
Fairie, William.......... 5
Fundenburg, Henry........ 3
Feester, Andrew.......... 8
Frost, Joseph............ 4
Farrar, Field............ 8.
Findley, John............ 6.
Fulgim, Jesse............ 2
Findlay, John............ 3.
Free, Adam...............10.

Gibson, William.......... 6.
Gradick, Jacob........... 8
Gradick, Jacob, Jr....... 4
Gibson, Jacob............10.
Gowen, Daniel............ 6
Gowen, Alex.............. 9
Gowen, Henry............. 5
Gladden, William......... 7
Gibson, Gervais.......... 6
Goodrum, John............ 5
Gladden, John............ 7
Gladden, Jesse........... 8
Goodrum, Allen........... 5
Goodrum, Thomas.......... 8
Gibson, Isaac............ 9
Gibson, Jacob............ 2
Garrett, Seth............ 2
Graig, Henry............. 4
Grant, Lewis............. 4
Graham, Isaac............ 8
Grigg, John.............. 9
Ginn, Jesse.............. 4
Goin, John............... 5
Garrett, Sarah........... 3
Goin, Jesse.............. 4
Gibson, Wilson........... 5
Gray, William............ 8
Gladney, Thomas.......... 7
Gladney, Richard.........10
Gibson, Randle........... 5
Gamble, James............ 5
Gladney, Samuel.......... 7

Gladney, Patrick......... 4	Hancock, Rachel.......... 2.	Ivery, Burril............ 1
Gamble, Samuel........... 4	Hunt, Hezekiah........... 6	Ivery, Henry............. 6
Gamble, Hugh............. 5	Hannah, James............13	Ivey, John............... 1
Gatewood, John........... 5	Harkins, Daniel O........ 7	Ivey, Susanah............ 4
Gibson, Joseph........... 5	Hoy, James............... 9	Ingleman, Jacob.......... 3
Gibson, Abraham..........10	Hoy, Quintin............. 2	
Graves, James............ 5	Hodges, Benjamin......... 8	Jones, Patience.......... 4
Graham, William.......... 5	Haigwood, Hy............. 9	Johnston, William........ 7
Graves, William..........	Haigwood, William........ 3	Johnston, Charles........ 8
Gliot, John.............. 9	Hughs, Church............10	Jenkins, John............ 4
Garmany, Hugh............ 2	Hughs, Goodman........... 8	Jones, Benjamin.......... 9
Goates, Philip...........14	Hughs, Willians.......... 8	Johnson, Thomas.......... 7
Gibson, Jacob............12	Harrison, Reuben......... 6.	Johnson, Judith.......... 3
Grigg, Rebekah........... 3	Harrison, William........ 4.	Jones, Ralph............. 8.
Godfrey, Margrit......... 5	Holley, William.......... 7.	James, David............. 5
Gwin, John............... 7	Harbirt, John............ 5	James, Enoch............. 2.
Grubs, Enoch............. 9	Hood, Robert............. 3	Johnson, Reuben.......... 4
Grissum, John............ 7	Hoofman, Christopher.....11	Jones, James............. 5.
Gose, Aaron.............. 7	Huston, John............. 9	James, David............. 6
Gwyn, Thomas............. 3	Hopkins, William......... 3	James, David, Sr........ 3
Gregg, John..............11	Harbin, William.......... 9	Johnson, James........... 6.
Grey, Andrew............. 6.	Herbin, Jesse............ 9	Joiner, William.......... 4
Gray, John............... 5	Hoppough, Phillip........11	Jackson, William......... 3
Gray, Robert............. 3	Hopkins, Richard......... 7	Jennings, John........... 8
Gray, James.............. 4.	Hall, Zachariah.......... 2	Jones, Abraham........... 3
Glandon, Stephe..........10	Hill, William............ 9	Johnson, John............ 6
Green, Thomas............ 4	Hill, John............... 5.	Johnson, William......... 4
Gordon, Alex............. 4	Hill, Richard............ 5	Johnson, Samuel.......... 3.
Goin, Daniel............. 6.	Hill, Asaph.............. 1	Jones, Darling........... 5
Gregory, Samuel.......... 4	Heart, James............. 6.	Jones, David............. 9
Gibson, Stephen.......... 5.	Handley, Thomas.......... 8	Jones, Vincent........... 3
	Haigwood, Elisha.........10	Jones, Elias............. 6
Holley, Benoni........... 4	Hogan, James............. 7	Jennings, Robert......... 5
Havis, Jesse............. 5	Hogan, William........... 7	
Hill, William............ 1	Hendricks, James......... 6	Kennedy, William......... 7
Hamilton, John........... 5	Hendricks, Thomas........ 7	Kirkland, Samuel......... 2.
Hunter, Henry............ 9	Harriss, James........... 6	Kirkland, William........ 7
Hollis, James............ 9	Hendricks, William....... 9	Knighton, Thomas......... 8
Hollis, William.......... 6	Hill, Thomas.............11	Knighton, Isaac.......... 7
Hollis, Moses............ 8.	Haigwood, Lewis..........10	King, James.............. 3
Hollis, Ekijah........... 5	Heart, Fredrick.......... 6	King, John............... 9.
Hornsbie, Moses.......... 3	Huffman, Daniel.......... 7	Knighton, Moses.......... 8
Hall, John............... 8	Holsey, George...........11	Kelly, John..............10
Hellims, Joseph.......... 9	Harrison, Burr........... 5.	Kirkland, William........ 5
Hellims, Margaret........ 5	Hill, Thomas............. 2	Kirkland, Zachariah...... 5.
Hill, Richard............ 4	Hughs, William...........11	Kirkland, William........ 7.
Hughs, Thomas............ 2	Hodge, Thomas............ 7	Killpatrick, Robert......12
Henson, Barlet........... 8	Harrison, Benjamin....... 4.	Koon, Conrad............. 7
Henson, Robert........... 2	Holley, Benoni........... 2	Kennedy, Alex............15.
Hill, Mrs................ 8	Hill, Thomas............. 8	Kirkland, Francis........10
Henson, Obadiah.......... 9.	Howton, George........... 6	Kincaid, James........... 9.
Hollis, John............. 6	Hinds, Thomas............ 4	Kearnaghan, Robert....... 3
Heaning, James........... 7	Howard, James............ 9	Kincaid, Alex............ 4
Heaning, Michael......... 5	Hunt, James.............. 6	Karnaghan, William....... 2
Hamilton, David.......... 7	Hardage, James........... 3	Kitchens, Charles........ 1.
Hays, Mathews............ 6	Ham, John................ 7	Kelly, Sarah............. 5
Henry, John..............12	Hall, Thomas............. 1	Kitchens, Eli............11.
Havis, John.............. 8	Henson, Mary............. 6	Knighton, Josiah......... 4.
Hassen, George...........10.	Hansel, Richard.......... 4.	
Harriss, Victor.......... 9	Hussay, Isaac............ 9	Lewcy, George............ 7
Hartle, Henry............ 7	Hornsbie, John........... 7	Lee, Burril.............. 6
Hawthorn, James..........10		Littlejohn, Marcellus.... 4.
Hughs, Aaron............. 5	Irick, John Adam......... 7.	Leavin, William.......... 4

Leitner, George............10	McQuarters, Alex........ 5	Matthews, Sarah.......... 8
Lott, George.............. 9	McIntier, Andrew........ 3	Moore, Mrs................ 5
Layton, Francis........... 9	McNeel, Archibald....... 7	McGrow, John............. 2
Lewis, William............10.	McNeel, Henry........... 3	McGraw, Jacob............ 4
Lucas, James.............. 2	McMeekan, James......... 4	Martin, Robert........... 6
Lewis, Charles............ 7.	McGomery, David......... 2	Mulholland, Robert....... 8
Lewis, Elis,.............. 3	Martin, John............ 2	McKinnie, Samuel......... 6.
Long, John, Sr............ 3	Murph, Widow............ 6	Mickle, Joseph........... 6.
Long, James............... 7	Moreton, Andrew......... 5	Mickle, Widow............ 5.
Long, John, Jr............10	Martin, James........... 1	McDaniel, William........ 6.
Long, David...............11	McDowell, Andrew........ 6.	McFaddin, William........ 7
Listner, John.............13	Moberly, William, Sr....10	McDaniel, Charles........ 4
Landrum, Josiah........... 6	McDurman, Joseph........ 4	Millar, William.......... 6
Lavender, William......... 6	Moberly, Levy........... 4	McCreight, Matthew....... 7
Lowry, William............ 4	Manning, Ambroze........10	Moore, Henry............. 3.
Lindsay, Benjamin......... 6	Miles, Samuel........... 7	McKain, Katherine........ 4
Liles, Araminas...........11	Miles, Hardy............ 6	McKain, Alex............. 3
Lashly, John.............. 7	Meek, Thomas............ 5	McClurkin, John.......... 7
Laulin, Jonothan.......... 4	McBride, Robert......... 4	McMillan, Mary........... 4
Legoe, Maddern............ 9	McCoy, Henry............12	Miller, Abraham.......... 4
Lee, Isam................. 7	Martin, Francis......... 7	Maybry, Daniel........... 4
Lemly, Putter............. 7	Martin, William......... 3	Maybry, Mary............. 4.
Liles, William............ 5	Mills, Leonard.......... 5	Moore, Robert............ 9
Lowrie, Conrad............ 5	Murphy, Gracey.......... 5.	Motte, William...........10
Lamar, James.............. 5	Mansell, Robert......... 7.	Majors, Elijah...........10
Liles, Thomas............. 6	Moberly, Edw., Jr....... 8.	Moberly, Edw............. 7
Landsdale, Isaac.......... 5	McMorries, William, Jr.. 4.	Malone, William.......... 7
Lovejoy, Edw..............11	May, James.............. 5.	Malone, Thomas...........10.
Lewers, Thomas............ 4	McCaule, Thomas H....... 9.	Meadows, Thomas.......... 7
Low, Isaac................ 4	Moon, William........... 9	Mayfield, Samuel......... 6
Lindsay, Robert........... 5	McCreight, James........ 6.	McDaniel, Joseph......... 5.
Lewis, Jacob.............. 9.	McKinnie, Samuel........ 4.	Moberly, Colin........... 5
Lane, Mary................ 6	McGill, Robert.......... 3	McDaniel, John........... 4
Liles, Aramenas........... 8.	Miles, Francis.......... 7	Moberly, Micaijah........ 5
Love, Isaac............... 6.	Miles, Thomas...........11	Meadows, Edw............. 2
Lowrie, Edw............... 7	McCreight, Quintin...... 5	Moberly, William......... 6
Lowry, Gideon............. 4	McCreight, James........ 5	McCollum, James.......... 8
Lorry, Job................ 8	McCance, John...........11	Moberly, Thomas.......... 7
Leech, John............... 4	Means, John............. 6.	Morst, Jacob............. 5
Long, John, Sr............10	McDaniel, Hugh.......... 3.	Moberly, William......... 6.
Long, John, Jr............ 3	Millar, Mrs............. 5.	McMurray, James.......... 6
Laughon, James............ 2.	Muse, Thomas............ 8.	Moberly, Samuel..........11
Lewis, James..............10.	Mattocks, John.......... 3	Meadows, Job............. 7
Lucas, John............... 3	Morgan, George.......... 6	Means, Thomas............ 4.
	Marr, James............. 6	Millar, James............ 7
Mann, James............... 8	Mickle, John............ 8.	Macon, Heartwell.........10
Morris, James............. 4	Muse, Widow............. 4.	Macon, Henry............. 9
Martin, Edw............... 5.	McKinnie, John.......... 6.	McCoy, Daniel............ 2
McGraw, Edw...............10	McDaniel, John.......... 1	McMorries, William, Sr...6
McGraw, David, Jr......... 7	Maynard, Edw............ 6	Martin, William.......... 1
McCants, Robert........... 5	Meredith, Thomas........ 7.	Morriss, John............ 1
McCreight, Robert......... 8	Millar, John............ 4	Morgan, Christopher...... 6
Martin, Robert............ 5.	McFaddin, John.......... 1	Morgan, William.......... 5
Martin, David............. 2	McDaniel, Daniel........ 1	Mansell, Robert.......... 5
Milling, Hugh............. 7	Martin, Henry........... 1	Martin, Robert........... 5
McMulland, James.......... 6	Moore, John............. 1	Marple, Thomas........... 3.
Major, John............... 4	Martin, Mary............ 7	McGraw, Benj............. 7
Milling, Jean............. 5.	Mt. Gomery, Hugh........ 8	Mooty, Joseph............ 7
McCreight, David..........10	Mt. Gomery, Chas........ 9.	McKinney, Benj........... 4
McDowell, Alex............ 5	McTyre, Frizle.......... 7.	Majors, Benj............. 5
Major, Nathaniel.......... 2	McCaimy, John........... 8	
McMullan, Thomas.......... 3.	McClintock, William..... 6	Nolland, Shad............ 7
McQuarters, Huston........ 3		Nolland, Steven.......... 7

Neat, Jacob............10	Parton, Philemon......... 8	Rogers, Henry...........11
Neel, Ann............... 5	Partin, Benjamin......... 4	Richardson, John......... 7
Neelie, James............ 1	Parks, John............. 7	Randolph, James.......... 5
Neely, Victor............ 5	Parnel, William..........15	Randolph, William........ 5
Neelie, Richard..........11	Parker, John............. 7	Robertson, Alex......... 7.
Neel, John............... 4	Porter, Thomas........... 3	Rachel, George........... 1
Nisbett, Samuel.......... 5	Peirson, Jeremiah........ 2	Roberts, Aaron.......... 8
Nettles, Zachariah....... 8	Perry, Samuel............ 8.	Rogers, William.......... 1
Nelson, Teague........... 1	Perry, Lewis............. 6	Robert, Richard.......... 4
Nelson, Thomas........... 9	Perry, Jesse............. 9	Rudd, George............. 8
Nelson, William.......... 7.	Pettypool, William....... 1	Robertson, Jane.......... 5
Nix, Edw................. 9	Pettywood, Henry......... 6.	Rabb, William...........10.
Nevit, William........... 6.	Payne, Zachariah......... 5.	Rabb, Joseph............. 9.
Neilson, James...........12.	Payne, Archibald......... 1.	Ringer, Nicholas......... 3
Noland, William.......... 6	Perkins, Widow........... 3	Reynolds, Hugh........... 8
Nelson, Henry............11	Pettypool, Ephraim....... 4.	Ratcliff, Widow......... 4.
Noland, Susanah.......... 5	Powell, William.......... 5	
Noland, James............ 3	Peay, Nicholas........... 4.	Starns, Peter............ 4
Nelson, Thomas........... 2		Shedd, Thomson, Shedd.... 2
Neese, Doras............. 6	Quarrell, Joseph......... 5	Strhother, Mrs........... 5.
Nevit, William Miles..... 5.		Shaver, Philip.......... 4.
	Reily, Bryant............ 3	Spence, Charles.......... 1
Owens, Joseph............ 5	Reily, Philip............ 7	Smith, Jacob............. 7
Owens, John.............. 1	Robertson, John.......... 9	Smith, William...........11
Owens, James............. 8	Rabb, Robert.............10.	Splan, Stephen........... 5
Owens, Benjamin.......... 3	Richardson, Robert....... 3	Sanders, Nathan.......... 5
Owens, Smallwood.........11	Roberts, Richard......... 4	Shirley, Robert.......... 4
O'Brient, Jesse.......... 5	Robinson, Thomas......... 5	Splon, John.............. 8
Owens, Benjamin.......... 4.	Roadin, Jeremiah......... 5	Sanders, John............ 3
Owens, William........... 9	Roadin, Leonard.......... 4	Sloan, John.............. 4
O'Neal, Edmund........... 6	Robinson, William........ 5	Sant, Thomas............. 7
Oister, John............. 2	Robinson, Mary........... 4	Stinson, John............ 3
	Reed, Robert............. 9	Smith, James............. 5
Powell, Lewis............ 3	Reed, William............ 6	Shelton, David........... 7
Parrot, Thorp............ 7	Rosborough, Alex......... 7	Simonds, Samuel.......... 8
Patterson, Peter......... 4	Robinson, John........... 7	Stanton, Joseph.......... 9
Powell, Cabel............ 6	Russell, James, Jr....... 7	Smithwick, William....... 8
Pigg, Edw................13	Russell, James, Sr....... 6	Smith, Matthew........... 4
Pigg, Charles............ 1	Rugely, Henry............ 5.	Sutton, John............. 8.
Pickett, Micaijah........10.	Robertson, John.......... 8.	Scott, James 8
Pickett, Charles......... 7	Richardson, Thomas....... 3	Seal, Thomas............. 5
Paul, James.............. 2.	Richardson, William...... 8	Starks, Turner........... 2.
Porter, John............. 3	Russell, William......... 3	Starks, Thomas........... 6.
Pair, John............... 6	Robertson, Robert........ 7	Smith, Thomas............11
Parks, James............. 7	Richardson, Samuel.......5.	Scott, Benjamin.......... 1
Phillips, Robert, Jr..... 8	Robertson, Alex.......... 8	Shain, John.............. 5
Phillips, Jean........... 3	Robertson, Alex, Jr...... 8	Spradley, Andrew......... 5
Paul, Archibald.......... 5	Ray, John................ 3	Sims, Joseph.............13
Pierson, James........... 6	Richman, John............ 7.	Stag, John............... 3
Perry, James............. 6	Robertson, Henry......... 8	Sanders, John............ 6
Patterson, Reuben........ 7	Rachel, Valentine........ 1	Stark, Reuben............ 4.
Porter, James............ 5	Rogers, John............. 5	Smith, Hermon............ 4
Peay, George............. 7.	Roberts, Nicholas........ 9	Smith, Charles........... 7
Peay, Austin............. 1	Robertson, William....... 8.	Sanders, Nathan.......... 6.
Procter, Samuel.......... 2.	Rayford, Philip.......... 9.	Sanders, Henry........... 8
Parrot, Thomas........... 5.	Roach, William...........12.	Stone, Thomas............11
Parrot, Thomas, Sr....... 3.	Rawls, Jesse............. 2	Stone, John.............. 1
Peaige, Henry............ 6	Rawls, Luke.............. 4	Stone, James............. 1
Phillips, James.......... 8	Rutland, James........... 8	Smith, Barlet............ 5
Pritchard, Charles....... 3	Robertson, Henry......... 7.	Smith, Hugh.............. 5.
Pearson, Mary............ 5.	Robertson, William....... 8.	Stedman, John............ 6
Patton, David............ 5	Robertson, John.......... 4	Stokes, Thomas........... 7
Pool, Walter............. 6	Rabb, James..............10	Shrub, Benjamin.......... 4
Parks, William........... 3	Rogers, James............ 6.	Stone, Elisabeth......... 5

Smith, Hampton,........... 6
Smith, Jesse.............. 5
Smith, Abner.............. 4.
Smith, Patrick, Sr........ 2
Smith, Patrick, Jr........ 4
Smith, Thomas............. 9
Steel, James.............. 3
Shedd, George,............ 5
Siberly, John............. 5
Smith, John............... 8
Simmonds, Edw............. 3
Summersall, William....... 7
Smith, Stephen............12
Smith, James.............. 4
Smith, Elisabeth.......... 3
Scott, William............ 7
Shannon, Thomas........... 5
Seal, Charles............. 5
Sims, Benjamin............ 5.
Seal, Elijah.............. 1
Sims, Edw................. 8
Seal, Anthony............. 7.
Simonds, Randolp.......... 5,
Simonds, Jesse............ 4
Swett, John............... 6
Stewart, John............. 7
Sims, John................ 6.
Swillaw, John............. 6.
Stuart, Alex.............. 6.
Smith, Moses.............. 2

Thompson, Richard......... 2
Turnapseed, Jacob......... 5.
Turnapseed, Bat........... 6.
Tidwell, William.......... 8
Tidwell, Edmond...........11
Tidwell, John.............11
Tidwell, Elli............. 7
Tidwell, William.......... 3
Tidwell, Robert...........13
Tidwell, Perry............ 2
Tucker, Simon............. 2
Thompson, David........... 6
Thompson, David........... 2
Thompson, Elisabeth....... 2
Thompson, William......... 5
Turner, John..............11.
Turner, John, Jr.......... 4
Turner, James............. 8
Terry, Amey............... 1
Thomas, Susanna........... 7.
Trap, John................ 4.
Trapp, William............12
Thompson, Nathan.......... 3
Taylor, Champ............. 3
Taylor, Jeremiah.......... 2
Taylor, Richard........... 7
Tidwell, Rachel........... 5
Taylor, Robert............ 5
Taylor, John.............. 4.
Turner, Widow............. 5
Thomson, Thomas........... 6

Thomas, Anderson..........13
Tidwell, Robert, Jr...... 9.

No one listed with the last
name beginning with "U"

Verce, Ezekiah............ 4
Vaughn, Thomas............ 8.

Willingham, William....... 3
Walker, Robert............ 6
Walker, John.............. 7
Woodward, Mrs. Elisabeth. 6.
White, Jesse.............. 7
Walker, Robert, Sr........6
Whitehead, John...........2
Williams, Joshua.......... 7
Watts, John...............10
Watts, Thomas............. 2
Winn, Richard.............10.
Welldon, Samuel...........10
Whitehouse, Thomas....... 2.
Wyret, Hermon............. 3
Wilson, William........... 7
Winn, Minor............... 3.
Winn, James............... 2.
Winn, John................ 2
Winn, John, Sr............ 8
Wallace, Jesse............ 8
Watson, John.............. 3
Wolf, Michael............. 9
Wilson, Elisabeth......... 4
Waugh, Samuel............. 4
Watson, Elisabeth......... 5
Watson, John.............. 2
Watson, Lucy.............. 2
Wright, Boland............ 3
Wooley, Richard...........10
Wilkerson, John...........6
Wilkerson, Robert......... 7
Wallis, Jesse T........... 4
Woodward, William......... 6.
Woodward, John............ 6.
Woodward, Richard.........12
Wright, William........... 5
Winn, John................ 7
Wilson, Theophilus........ 7
Wootan, Aaron............. 7
Wootan, Moses............. 7
Watts, George............. 13
Willingham, William....... 3.
Willingham, John.......... 4.
Wells, William............ 4
Wayne, George............. 5
Ward, John................ 7
Williams, John............ 3
Ward, Robert.............. 3
Willingham, Thomas........ 7
Wooten, Daniel............ 3.
Waugh, Samuel............. 6.
William, Thomas........... 4
Williams, John............ 3

Whitehouse, Thompson..... 2
Weaver, Morriss........... 6.
Woodward, John............ 6
Woodward, Burbage......... 2
Watts, Edw., Sr........... 9
Wilson, Robert............ 2
Workman, James............ 5
Walker, John.............. 1
Wilson, Jesse............. 9
Wilson, James............. 6.
Wooten, John.............. 5.
Wilson, Joel.............. 4
Wilson, John..............10.
Wooten, John.............. 5.
Wilson, Joel.............. 4

Wilson, James............. 3
Wells, Samuel............. 5
Winchister, Willoughby...10
Wells, Joseph............. 5
Williamson, Roland........ 5.
Williamson, Lemual........ 4
Williamson, Charles....... 6
Williamson, Sterling...... 2
Williamson, Abagail....... 3

Yarbrough, William........ 5
Young, Andrew............. 8.
Young, Mary............... 5
Young, Samuel............. 5.
Yarbrough, Richard........ 8
Yarboro, Owen............. 5
Young, Hugh............... 4.
Yarboro, William.......... 4
Yarbro, Thomas G.......... 1
Yarbrough, John........... 7

INDEX

-A-

ADAMS, Miss 63
AIKEN, David, 76,79; Eliza, 79
    James, 14; Joe. 76;
    J.B., 8, 73;
ALSTON, Agnes, 72; Anne. 72,73;
    Charnel, 72; Col. 71; David, 72,73;
    Elizabeth M., 70,73; Fannie K., 79
    James, 31,70,71,72,73;
    James Henry, 71; John, 73, John, Sr., 72;
    Joseph Kirkland, 72; Kirkland, 71;
    Mrs., 71; Margaret, 72, 75;
    Marion Kennan, 71; Mary, 72; Samuel, 7, 72;
    Mrs. Susan, 72; Col. Wm. J., 70, 71, 72, 73, 79;
    William J., 6, 31; W.J., 8; Wm. L., 73;
    William Samuel, 71, 72;
ANDERSON, Edward, 69; Thomas, 69
ARMSTRONG, Mr., 69;
ARNETTE, John Q., 45; Dr. R.C., 45;
    Susan T., 42;
ARNOLD, William, 57
ATKINS, 45
AXUM, Patsie, 78;

-B-

BAKER, 15
BALAR, Captain, 64
BARKLEY, 13; Pugh, 9; Jas., 7,9,
    John, 9
    Robert, 31
    Samuel G., 31
BARNWELL, R.W., 5
BEALES, 46
BEAM, Edith, 45
    Martin, 53
BEATY, Archibald, 9
BLAIR, General, 31
BLOCKER, 16
BONNER, I, 7
BOOKTER, Thomas, 23
BOOTAU, Major, 74
BOULWARE, Alben, 47
BOYCE, Mrs., 36,37;
    Alexander, 35
    John, 35
    Mrs. Lydia Waters, 35
    Robert, 35
    W.W., 7,8,35,73,75
    William Waters, 35
BOYD, Mry Mary, 72, 73
    Miss, 62
BOYLES, J.R., 9
BOYLESTON, Dr., 20
    R.D., 8
BRADSHAWS, 18
BRANNAN, James, 45

BRATTON, Dr., 14
    General John, 7,8,77
    W.M., 8
    Wm. H., 7, 75
BRICE, T.S., 8
BROOM, Capt. Billy, 75
BROWN, 15
    Marianna, 71
    Miss, 39
    Colonel Newton, 39
    William, 7
BUCHANAN, Ann, 32
    Calvin, 34
    Creighton, 29, 30, 33, 34
    Dr. B.A., 81
    Eliza, 34
    Buchanan's Ford, 30
    Capt. John, 28, 29, 30
    John, 6, 7, 33, 64, 71
    General John, 30, 31, 32
    John M., 75
    J.R., 9
    John R., 29
    Martha, 33, 34
    Rachel, 30, 33
    Robert, 28, 33, 34
BURT, Armisteed, 5
BUTLER, George, 40
BYNUM, Capt. Thomas, 23

-C-

CALHOUN, John C. 7, 60
CALMUS, Miss, 68
CAMERON, Alex, 42, 43
    Dr. Andrew S., 42
    J. Feaster, 42
    James, 42
    John, 42
    Robert, 42
    Robert Gregg, 38, 42
    Sarah, 43
CARLISLE, Prof. James R., 29
    Capt. John, 29
    Rev. William, 29
CATHCART, Charles, 20
    John N., 20
CAUTHEN, Mrs., 75
CHAMBERS, Aleck, 20
CHAPMAN, 47, 49.
    Giles, 49
    John, 49
CLARK, Capt. 30
    Dr. Caleb, 78
    H.H., 8
    Matthies, 78
CLAY, Henry, 5
CLINTON, Sir Henry, 56
CLOUD, Dr. William, 47
CLOWNEY, Moses, 53
    R.C., 8
    S.B., 9

COBDEN, , 36
COCKRELL, J., 9
    John, 50, 76, 77
    John Easter, 43
    Moses, 43
COLCOCK, C.J., 5
COLEMAN, Ancil 45
    Andrew, 46
    Allen L., 45
    Allen, 40
    Dr. B.F., 41
    Betsy, 45
    Dr. Bob, 40
    Charles, 45
    David A., 41
    David H., 46
    David Roe, 38, 40, 41, 44, 45, 46
    Elizabeth, 41, 45, 46,
    G.W., 40, 41
    Griffin R., 45
    Francis, 45
    Dr. Franklin, 40
    Hattie E. (nee Porter), 39
    Henry A., 41
    Henry Jonathan, 40, 41, 45, 54
    H.J., Jr., 41
    Hiram, 48
    H.J.F.W., 44
    Isaac, 43
    Isabelle, 38, 42, 46
    Jacob F., 40
    John R., 44
    John C., 46
    J.A.F., 41
    Jonathan D., 44, 50
    Martin, 45
    Dr. Preston, 40, 41
    Rebecca, 45
    Robert, 44, 45, 46,
    Robert C., 41
    Robert F., 40
    Robert H., 40
    Dr. R.W., 40
    Sarah, 41, 45, 46
    Robert Roe, 44
    Sarah, 41, 45, 46
    Solomon, 45
    Stephen, 45
    Thomas, 49
COLEMAN, Wiley, 48, 54
    Wiley F., 46
    Wiley R., 44
    William, 45
    William, "Buck", 44
    Wilson H., 46
    Zerabable, 45
COLVIN, Andy Feaster, 47
    William, 38
CONWAY, 47
COOK, P.B., 7
    John, 64

Dr. John, 81
N.P., 31
Gen. Philip, 72
Susan P., 72
COOPER, Adam, 38
    Eve, 38
    George, 43
    Margaret, 43
    Margaret Fry, 38
CORNWALLIS, Lord, 3
CREIGHTON, William, 32
CROCKETT, Davy, 80
CROSSWHITE, Frances, 56
CROWDERS, 49
CROSBY, Charles, 47
    Coleman, 47
    D., 8
    Davis, 47
    D.P., 46
    Mrs. D.P., 47
    Richard, 47
    Stephen, 47, 49
    Thomas, 47
    W.W., 47
    William, 47
CUSHING, Gen. Caleb., 36

-D-

DANSBY, Daniel, 59
DANTZLER, Cornelia M, 79
    Georgianna C., 25
    J.M., 25
    Mary A., 73
    Col. Olin M., 73, 79
DAVIS, A.E., 26
    Benj., 63
    Miss Celia, 62
    Cline C., 63
    Franklin, 59
    Glenn, 63
    Harriett, 63
    Henry C., 6, 8
    Col. J. Bunyan, 63
    J.B., 9
DAVIS, James, 56
    James B., 59
    Dr. James B., 62
    Jeff, 20
    Gen. Jeff C., 12
    John, 56
    Col. John, 62, 63
    Jonathan, 63
    Col. Jon. 63
    Colonel Jonathan, 59, 62
    Mary Glenn, 64
    R. Meene, 4
    Nathan, 43
    Rebecca, 64
    Major Wm. J., 63
    Wm. K., 59, 63

de GRAFFENREID, C. 59
DOUGLAS, A.S., 8
  Charles, 47
  Charles A., 8
DUNOVANT, Miss Kate, 80
DYE, "Guber", 53
DYES, 46
DURHAM, Capt. Charnal, 55
DUVAL, L.W., 9

-E-

EARLE, Miss, 23
EDRINGTON, A.L., 56
  Elizabeth, 58
  Francis, 57
  Francis H., 49
  Golding, 23
  Harrison, 57
  Henry Clay, 57
  James, 57
  James F., 57
  Jas. P., 57
  John, 57
  Mildred, 57
  Miss Mollie, 62
  Robert J., 57
  Sallie, 58
  William, 55, 57
  William H., 57
ELAM, Miss, 46
ELKIN, Bayliss, 65
  Bayliss E., 8
  David, 65
  David R., 65
  Major Elliott, 65
  James, 65
  J. Bunyan, 66
  Rev. Wm., 65
ELLIOTT, James M., 9
  J. McKinney, 34
ELLISON, Emmett, 54
  Robert, 4
  R.E., 9
ELMORE, F.H., 5
ERVIN, Dr., 68
ESTES, Mrs. Dr. 47
EVANS, David, 8, 9
  David R., 7, 14, 15
  D.R., 7, 14, 15
  D.R., Jr., 14
  John H., 7
  John, 14
  Joseph, 14
  Mrs., 14

-F-

FANT, Dr. F.H., 57
  Dr. F.M., 60
  Dr. F.M.E., 57
  F.W., 57
  Jessie, 57
  John, 57
  O.H.P., 57
  Dr. Sam, 57
  William, 24, 57
  Willie, 57
FEASTER, Andrew, 38, 39, 40, 43, 49
  Capt. Andrew, 9
  Belle, 40
  Capt., 10
  Chaney, 38, 41
  D.R., 39, 41, 49
  David R., 39
  Edith D., 39
  Elbert H., 39
  Jacob, 38, 43
  Jacob N., 40
  Jacob, (Squire Jake) 38, 46
  John, 38, 39, 40, 41, 42, 45, 49
  John C., 27, 39
  John M., 38, 42
  Julia, 40
  Laurens, 38, 47
  Mary, 38, 40
  Mary N., 39
  Moses, 38
  Narcissa M., 40
  Nathan A., 39
  Peter, 38
  Sallie, 40
  Savilla, 38
  Susan, 38 40
  Susan E., 39
  T.D., 39. 46
FEE, Mrs. L.R., 49
FERGUSON, Stephen, 13
FINNEGAN, General, 74
FITZ HUGH, 55
FOOT, Miss, 22
FORD, John, 63
  Mrs. Robert, 11, 12
  Mr. Robert, 12, 13
FRANKLIN, Miss, 46
FREE, Simeon, 48
FULLER, Miss, 63
FURMAN, Rev. James C., 62, 63, 64
FURNEY, 56
  , Nancy, 65

-G-

GADSDEN, Christopher, 81
GAILLARD, Frances B., 37
  Henry A., 7
  H.A., 8
  Richard W., 37

GAITHER, Rachael, 17, 18
    Richard, 17
GELSTON, James, 53
GIBSON, Jacob, 64
    Capt. Tully S., 75
    Mrs., 75
GILDER, Dr. James K., 57
GILMERS, 58
GLADDEN, Miss, 40
    James, 45
    John, 45
GLENN, Blanton, 23
    Col. John, 68
GODFREY, Margaret, 24
GOODLETT, Col. S.D., 27
GOREE, (Widow), 23
GRANT, President U.S., 8
GRAY, John, 64
GRIFFIN, George, 56
GWINNS, 48

-H-

HALL, Col. Alexander B., 68
    Jane, 68
    Mary, 68
HALSELL, Dorcas, 48
HAMILTON, James, Jr., 5
HANAHAN, Dr., 16
HANCOCK, Andrew, 45
    John, 53
    Robert, 64
HARDEN, John, 33
    T., 33
HARPER, Chancellor, 5, 23
    William, 6
HARRINGTON, Miss, 23
HARRIS, Dr., 57
    Mr., 68
HARRISON, John, R., 81
HASKELL, Col. A.C., 3
HAVIS, J., 7
    Col. Jesse, 15
HAYNE, Gov. R.Y., 5, 24
    Robert Y., 5
HAYNESWORTH, Sallie A., 27
    Miss Sue, 68
HEATH, Miss Alice, 73
    Thomas, 81
HELLER, Silas, H., 60
HELM, 55
HENDERSON, David, 48
HERBERT, Mrs., 37
HEBRON, Mrs. R.A., 14
HENRY, Mrs., 79
HILL, Col., 68
    "London Bill", 53
    Sallie, 65

    Simeon, 43, 44
    "Stump Bill", 53
    "Varmint Dick", 53
    Capt. William E., 43
HILLS, 83
HODGES, Mr., 59, 60
HOFFMAN, Mrs. (nee Robinson), 42
HOLMES, H., 66
HORLBECK, Dr., 19
HUDSON, J.W., 4
HUGENIN, C.J., 63
HUGER, Daniel E., 5
HUGHES, Dave, 75
    Frank, 75
    Henderson, 75
    Robert, 75
HUNTER, G.B., 7
    James Levy, 42
HUTCHISON, William P., 59

-I-

IREY, Cora

-J-

JACKSONS, 16-a
JACKSON CREEK CHURCH, 33
JACOBS, Shedrack, 9
JENKINS, 47
    "Thundering", 28
JETER, John, 43
    William, 43
JOHNSON, James, 9
    S., 7
    Samuel, 31
JOHNSTON, James, 54
    Job, 5
    Miss, 46
JOHNSTONE, Chancellor Job, 57
JONES, Lizzie, 57

-K-

KELLER, 81
KENNEMORE, 43
KERR, Miss Fannie D., 49
    William, 49
    W.H., 9
KINCAID, Elizabeth, 69
    Capt. James, 62
    James, 66, 67, 68
    Colonel, 69
    Nancy, 68, 69
    Rebecca, 62
    Colonel William, 68
KINARD, M.L., 27
    Mrs., 58

KINNERLY, Mrs., 22
KIRKLAND, Frances, 70,71,72, 73
      Joseph, 64,70,
      J.D., 8
      William, 64,70
KIRKLANDS, 70
KIRKPATRICK, John 69

         -L-

LYLES: Colonel Aromanos, 22,24,64
      Austin, 26
      Belton, 26
      Benjamin, 23
      Carrie, 26
      Drucilla, 23,24
      Eliza, 23
      Eliza R., 25
      Ephriam, 22,24,56
      "Little" Ephriam, 22, 23
      Esther, 80
      E.F., 9
      Fannie, 57
      Fannie Eliza, 27
      Fannie Hortensia, 27
      Florence 27
      Henry J., 39
      Capt., 26
      James, 22,26
      Capt. James, 23
      J.C., 46
      John, 22,23,24,26
      Col. John, 22
      John W., 26
      John S., 8
      J. Feaster, 26
      Mrs., 25
      Major, 58
      Mattie P., 26
      Mary C., 27
      Nicholas, 26
      Rebecca, 22, 23
      Rebecca V., 26,79
      Ruth, 38
      Sue Boykin, 26
      Sue H., 27
      Sallie, 26
      Miss Sallie, 39
      Thomas, 7,22,24,26,78
      Capt. Thomas, 5, 26,
      Capt. Thos. M., 25,26,79,
      Major, 25
      Major Thomas, 24,27,56,59,80
      T.W., 46
      Thomas Jefferson, 23
      Valentine, 22,23
      William, 27
      William H., 27

      Major William S., 47
      William ("Carpenter Bill") , 23
      William Boykin, 25
      William S., 6,25,71,78
      Mrs. William S., 71
      Colonel William S., 39
      Major William, 27

         -M-

MACONS, 48
MADDEN, Dr., 19,20
MANNING, R.J., 5
      Thomas L., 42
MARTIN, Edward, 64
MATTHEWS, Miss Edith, 72
MAY, Benjamin, 64
MAYFIELD, Mrs. Wesley, 40,42,45
MAYO, Thompson, 65
McAFIE, Lee, 43
McCALL, J.B., 6
      John B., 31
McCANTS, J.B., 8, 75
      J. Wm., 26
McCAULE, Rev. T.R., 4
McCLANAHAN, Miss, 39
McCONNELL, Andrew, 47,54,
      A.J. (Dick), 42
      Nancy, 41
McCORLEY, John D., 9
McCREIGHT, James 19, 29

McCULLY, 19

McDOWELL, D., 8
McDUFFIE, George, 5
McGHEES, 23
McGILL, Thomas, 62
McKARNEY, Mr., 65
McKINSTRY, John, 75
      Nancy, 75
      Samuel, 75
      Thomas S., 8,75
McLANE, Jonathan, 53
McLEMORE, 79
McLURKIN, Dr., S.W.B., 46
McMAHAN, Daniel, 68
      James, 68
      John, 68
McMANUS, 56
McMASTER, Mrs., 21
      George, 14
      George H., 3, 67
      G.R., 8, 29
      John, 16-a, 19
      Mrs. Rachael, 34
McMEEKIN, Hayne, 8
      Rosalie, 26
McMORRIS, William, 64

McMULLEN, Mr., 34
McSHAN, Andy, 43
    Ferdinand, 43
    Hundley, 43
    Judith, 43
McWHORTER, William, 49
MEADORS, 46
Meador, John, 47
    Dr. Lem, 47
    Meredith Poole, 47
    Dr. W.M., 47
MEANS, 22
    David, 31
    David H., 6,8
    John H., 8,59
    John, 30
    Colonel John, 6,7
    Gen. John, H., 61
    Gov. John H., 47
    Ned, 53
    Robert, 31,59
    Thomas, 30,31,
    Col. Thomas, 22
    William B., 59
MELTONS, 54
METCALF, 55
MILLERS, 21
MILLER, Stephen D., 5
MILLIKEN, Mary, 33
MILLING, David, 31
    Capt. Hugh, 15,30,33
    John, 8,9
    Mary, 30
    Sallie Burney, 30
    Sarah, 30
MITCHELL, Beverley C., 41
MOTLEY, 81
    Cullen, 47,49
    David, 81
    Drucilla, 38
    Isham, 49
    James B., 68
    John G., 17
    "Cage" (Michajah), 47,49,53
    Notly, 49
    Robert, 50
    Samuel, 38
    Gemimah, 53
MONTGOMERY, David, 7
MOORE, Major Henry, 28
    Rev. Mrs., 49
    Sheriff, 10
    William, 9
MORRIS, Sue C., 26
MOUNT ZION SOCIETY, 14
MURDOCKS, 48
MUSE, James, 9
MYERS, J.J., 8
    Wm. M. 59

-N-

NEIL, J.J., 9
NELSON, Wm., 9
NEVITT, Brooks, 49
    Cornelius, 47,49
    Francis, 47,49
    Jack, 49
    Joseph K., 49
    Laura, 49
    Precious Ann 49
NEWBLES, 47
NOLAN, Isaac, 46
NORRIS, Mary, 39

-O-

OBEAR, Rev. J., 19
OLLIVER, E.W., 9
O'NEAL, John B., 5
    Richard, Sr., 65
OWENS, Albert W., 73
    Alston, 73
    Anne, 74
    James, 73,74
    James, Sr., 74.75
    James B., 74
    Jesse, 73,74,75,81
    J.T., 8
    Mary, 73
    Dr. Sam, 76
    Samuel, 73.75
    S.B., 8
    Wm., 73,75,77
    Dr. William, 76,77
    Gen. Wm., 74

-P-

PALMER, Rev. Edward, 32
    Edward G., 6,7,8,31,73,75
PARKS, Miss, 47
PARR, Major Henry W., 66
PARROTT, Nathan, 53
PEARSON, Mrs., 70
    Mrs. Elizabeth, 35
    Mrs. D., 70
    G.B., 27
    George B.,Dr., 16-a. 35,5
    Grace, 66
    John, 65
    Gen. John, 64 ,65,66
    Martha, 65
    Mary E., 35
    Philip, 65
    Philip, Sr., 60
    F.B., 7,78
    Rebecca, 78

PEAY, A.F., 7
    Col. Austin F., 25
    N.A., 7
PERRY, B.F, 5
PFISTER, see Feaster
PHILLIPS, James, 33
    Capt. James, 33
    Col. John, 34
    Robert, 33
    Smith, 33
PICKETTS, 16-a
PICKETT, John, 17
    Keziah, 38
    Micajah B., 41
    Reuben, 17
PLAYER, T., 7
POELINITZ, Lt., F.A., 26
POOLLNITZ, Lou, 26
POPE, Miss, 80
    James, 68
    Mr., 68
PORTER, Rev., C.M., 39
POWELL, Cullen, 59
PRESTON, Hon. W.C., 32

-R-

RAGSDALE, 44
RAWLS, B.A., 40
    Maria Louisa, 39
    Dr. T.J., 40
    Victoria E., 39
RHETT, R.B., 5
RICHARDS, Miss, 23
RICHARDSON, John B., 5
RION, Col. James, 3
ROBERTSON, Wm. B., 6,8,71
ROBINSON, Billy, 53
    Ed, 33
    John, 53
    Nat, 53
    Rebecca, 53
    Willie, 53
    William, 53
ROE, Elizabeth, 44
ROGERS, Rev. James, 62
    John, 62
ROOK, Katie, 23
RUFF, Silas, 9
RUSH, James, 65
RUTLAND, James, 75
    S.R., 8

-S-

SATTERWHITE, Richard, 58
SCOTT, Dr., 13
    Miss, 62

SECREST, Miss, 41
SEYMORE, Maj. William, 54
SHADY GROVE MEETING HOUSE, 16-a
SHEDD, J.N., 8
SHELTON, 47
SHERMAN, Gen., 3,11,12,13
SHIRLEY, Hatter John, 53
    Mirron, 53
SHIRLEYS, 53
SIMONS, S.M., 39
SIMS, Reuben, 23
SIMONTON, Dr. Christopher, 42,43
    John, 42,43
SIMPSON, Billy, 81
    John, 38,43
SLOAN, Miriam M., 27
SMART, Harriett, 79
    Dr. William, 75
SMITH, Dr., 66
    John, 24,59
    William, 6
STARKE, Jane, 79
    Reuben, 79
STEVENSON, Col. Hugh, 62
    Samuel H, 41
STEWARD, James S., 9
STONE, Elizabeth, 38
    Jacob, 38,47
    Margaret, 43
STROTHER, Capt. Dargen, 80
    John, 64
    J.D., 8
    Gen. William, 80
    Sallie, 81
    Sallie W., 25
    William, 4,64
STROUD, J.H., 13
SUMTER, General Thomas, 16-a, 22

-T-

TAYLOR, General Ed., 48
THOMPSON, O.R., 9
THOMAS, 47
    C.E., 8
TRIBBLE, Mr., 39
TRIPLET, 43
TUCKER, William, 43
    Starling, 80
TUPPER, Frederick, 63
TURNBULL, Robert J., 5
TURNER, 54
TYNES, Henry, 49

-V-

VALENTINE, 22
VANDERHORST, John, 3

VANCE, Carr E., 58
　　　L.L., 58
　　　Roseborough, 58
　　　Susan, 58
　　　Whitfield, 58
　　　William, 58

-W-

WAGNER, 48
WAGENER, Fort, 48
WALDO, Mrs. J.W., 73
WALKER, Miss, 47
WARDLAW, F.H., 5
WASHINGTON, President George, 66
WATERS, Charlie, 49
　　　Lydia, 35
　　　Oliver, 49
WATT, Mr., 76,77
WATSON, Capt., 64
WEBB, Elizabeth, 56
　　　Jesse, 56
WEIRS, 48
WELCH, John, 63
WHITNEY, 67
WIDENERS, 46
WILLIAMS, General, 20
　　　Tom, 48
　　　William, 40
WILLIAMSON, Alice, 78
　　　Martha, 81
　　　Roland, 81
WILSON, John L., 5
WINN, John, 3, 4
　　　Col. John, 15.34,64
　　　Minor, 15,34
　　　Gen. Richard, 3,7,14,15
　　　　　16, 16-a, 33
WITHROW, W.H., 5
WITHERS, Judge, 71
　　　Lawson, 49
WOLLING, John G., 39
WOOD, James R., 58
WOODWARD, 78
　　　Mary A., 25
　　　Billy, 52
　　　Cynthia, 78
　　　Edward, 80
　　　Esther, 78,79
　　　G.W., 9
　　　Hattie, 80
　　　Jemima, 81
　　　John, 80

　　　J.A., 7,8
　　　James A., 59
　　　Lucy, 81
　　　Mary, 80
　　　Mary Ann Collins, 79
　　　Mary Collins, 78,80, 8
　　　Osmund, 78,81
　　　Dr. Osmund, 79
　　　Rebecca, 81
　　　Regina, 81
　　　Richard, 9
　　　Sallie, 78,80
　　　Miss Sallie S., 74
　　　Sallie P., 27
　　　Thomas E., 59
　　　Thomas W., 7,8
　　　Major Thomas, 3,8,26,50,
　　　William, 7,31
　　　Wm. T., 80
　　　Col. William T., 78,79
WOOLEY, Col. A. Feaster, 43m
　　　E., 43
　　　Ezekiel, 9
WORTHY, William, 23
WRIGHT, Dr., 50
　　　Belin, 50
　　　David, 53
　　　Pinkey, 51,52
　　　William, 50,53
　　　Uriah S., 50,51,52

-Y-

YONGUES, 48
YOUNGUE, Harriet, 32
　　　A.W., 9
YOUNGEm John I., 42, Henry
　　　Henry, 42
　　　James W., 42
YOUNGUE, John M., 32
　　　Parson, 32
YONGUE, Parson S.W., 14
YOUNGE, Robert, 42
　　　Rebecca, 41
YONGUE, Sarah A., 41
　　　William, 42
　　　Samuel, 32
　　　Samuel W., 9
YOUNGESVILLE, 42

-Z-

ZIMMERMAN, Miss, 63

www.ingramcontent.com/pod-product-compliance
Lightning Source LLC
LaVergne TN
LVHW021410080426
835508LV00020B/2534